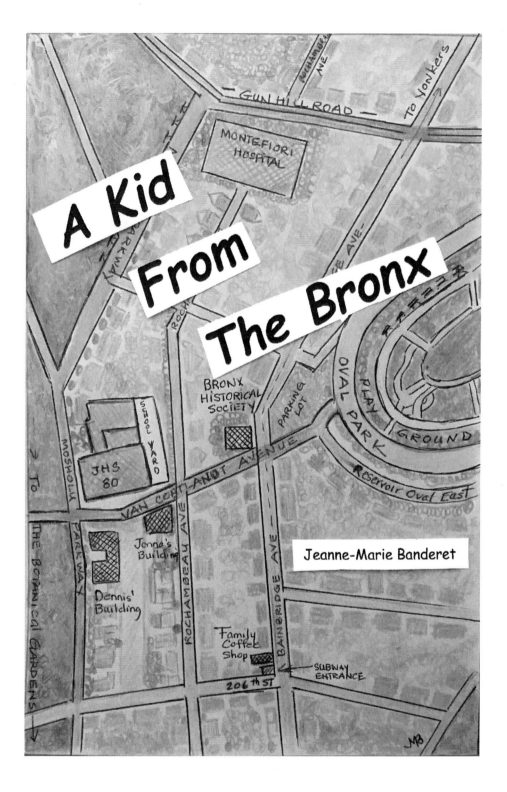

A Kid From The Bronx
The Early Years

Jeanne-Marie Banderet

Desert Wind Press

Cover Art and Map by Jeanne-Marie Banderet
Cover and Book Design by Robert Brent Gardner

Independently published by Desert Wind Press LLC
ISBN 978-1-956271-01-0 (print softcover)
Control:20211019.45218.206

This book is dedicated to my children, grandchildren, future great-grandchildren, extended family, loved ones and friends.

"The three components of happiness are something to do, someone to love and something to look forward to."

Gordon Livingston

Introduction from the Editor

History is personal to those who live it. Certainly, it was for Jeanne-Marie, the real Jonna. She wrote the book for several reasons. First, it was a gift to her kids and grandkids of what she went through in her early life and what that life was like a more than a half-century or so ago in the Bronx. My thought after reading and proofing several versions is that life is of interest and value to many, including residents of the Bronx, nostalgic oldsters, curious youngsters, some history buffs, and others.

Second, it was a long overdue introspection and catharsis to put her subsequent life in perspective and to reaffirm her humanness. I found Jonna's story refreshing and entertaining. It is easy to read and enjoy. There are elements of humor and of sadness and of the unusual that distinguishes one life from another.

Third, it was a challenge that she found meaningful. There were the challenges of writing to completion and the challenges of researching, and remembering, and reflecting accurately and honestly.

Blessings to Jeanne-Marie, to her Jonna, her family and her readers.

Don Heacox

Introduction

Through the times of our life, perspectives change. What seems evident from one angle, is quite different from another point of view. I learned about perspective during the many art classes I've taken throughout the years. With that in mind, the following memoire (memorandum, autobiography) is from the perspective of a young child, who I have called Jonna; a nickname often used by my family. It is intended to inform and entertain the reader with an honest and unbiased account of her life as she perceived it, along with oral stories and some research about the times to round it out.

Originally, it was intended as a history, not only of her time, but to include the earlier history of how the family developed starting from as far back as the turn of the century. Initially the memoire was to be left for my children, grandchildren, close friends, and possibly some interested acquaintances. However, my husband and faithful editor, suggested that it might appeal to a larger audience; perhaps older folks, people who grew up in the Bronx, people of Italian ancestry or others who might enjoy a nostalgic recollection of simpler, less complicated times.

The writing process turned out to be more challenging than I first thought. Starting around the end of 2018, I began reminiscing about the good old days, growing up in New York City. By the way many Manhattan dwellers consider the outer boroughs of NY, ie Staten Island, Queens, Brooklyn and the Bronx to be the suburbs. Upon reflection, I believe the Bronx was the best of both worlds. The neighborhood offered typical city convenience with all shopping, ethnic foods, and services within walking distance, even two movie theaters. What set it apart was the amount of green space and parks surrounding my particular neighborhood located in the northwest section of the Bronx near the Yonkers border.

As I embarked on this writing, during the past few years, I have come to appreciate that writing is truly an art form, drawing pictures with words, stirring the imagination of the reader, and drawing the reader into another world; another reality, if you will. Each one of our stories is unique; however, there exists a common thread of human experience that each reader can relate to. Herein lies the challenge. To tell a story, as honestly and true to experience as can be, while providing some history that is informative and engaging at the same time. Equally important is what experiences to include and to determine which are to be left out.

Maybe, and best of all, is that this journal has been a catharsis of sorts for me. Everyone has a story to tell, and in the telling, in the writing, insights and reflections are sorted out; the moving pictures in our minds are clearer, sharper, less confusing and ultimately simpler.

Finally, I have come to appreciate the Bible scripture Micah 6:8… "He has told you O man, what is good; and what does the Lord require of you but to do justice, and to love kindness and to walk humbly with your God."

Amen

Jeanne-Marie Banderet

Table of Contents

Part III

Part IV

Acknowledgments

First, I want to thank my husband, Don Heacox, for patiently reviewing and editing the writes and rewrites and corrections to the manuscript. He gave me the thumbs up on many of the chapters and encouraged me to go forward when I got frustrated. Thank you Don.

Next are the sources I used to add detail and clarity to the story. Teri at the library in the Mormon Church helped me trace the ancestry and family tree as far back as the turn of the century. Thank you Teri.

My cousin Dennis helped me remember some of the names and places I mention in the book. Thank you big Cuz

Internet searches like Wikipedia also provided some forgotten details and reinforced my memory. Thank you for providing easily accessible information.

Finally, the Bronx Historical Society, which I mention in the book, also provided historical archived information about the Bronx and the neighborhood I grew up in. Thank you all.

A special thanks to the publisher of this book, Robert Gardner, whose efficient and caring attitude got me through the process. Thank you Robert.

Part I

Grandma Arrives

Carmela Ferrara arrived on the American shores in the year 1899. She was among hundreds of thousands, if not millions of immigrants from all over Western Europe. During that time period, from about the 1850's to the 1920's, the Irish, the Jews and the Italians, including the Sicilians, would seek a better life and the wonderful prospect of becoming American citizens. They flocked to American soil for opportunity only this great free country could offer. Most times, however, they met with hardships, poverty, and poor living conditions.

After clearance from Ellis Island, most would assimilate into the NY lower Manhattan slums. Others with family ties found their way to New Jersey, Brooklyn, Queens or Staten Island which was called Richmond at that time. An attitude of bigotry and discrimination welcomed each new ethnic group. They were harassed by the police, landlords and other political groups who wished to maintain their power. By sticking together and putting up a united front, some made progress and assisted newcomers and newly arriving family members.

Some made their way early on and began operating small businesses, trade and craft services and cottage industries that provided a sustainable living. Among the Italians, The Black Hand or early Mafiosi, would extort weekly payment for protection. Fear of reprisal from the Black

Hand thugs, kept the shop owners dutifully paying weekly. Some would refuse to pay the vig on loans, and would find themselves or their families subject to physical abuse or worse. In spite of the set-backs, most families held out hope of better days and the freedom they desperately sought.

Grandma Carmela and her two sisters, Rose and Mary, found work in a cigar factory. There were no child labor laws back then, and many young children held these jobs. They sometimes worked 8-10 hour days rolling cigar leaves, clipped and sealed for a penny a piece. Most days they earned $1 each. Three dollars a day for 6 days would amount to about $18.00 per week or more. In the early 1900's that amount would be enough to sustain a family of 4 renting in a tenement, cold water flat apartment. Grandma Nina did not go out to work. She maintained the home and did some sewing for extra income. The three sisters turned over their paychecks to her. They were sometimes rewarded with some spending money for extras or a local show.

Other chores like laundry, meal preparation, mending clothes and shopping were also part of the family routine for youngsters at that time. Mandatory education was not strictly enforced. There weren't enough schools to accommodate the burgeoning population of youngsters in the immigrant communities.

While still in their native land of Sicily, Grandma Carmela, Aunt Rose and Aunt Mary attended a Catholic school for basic education to about the 8th grade. They learned to speak, read and write real Italian and were fluent in both Sicilian and proper Italian. They were not among the throngs of illiterate immigrants who entered the US. Those who owned land who were more prosperous could afford the tuition for their children. The Ferrara family owned some land that grew grapes, figs, tomatoes, herbs and other vegetables. Some exchanges were made with other families who grew wheat and grains. The local mill would grind the wheat and return the fine flour for baking. The aroma of freshly baked bread wafting through the air must have been fantastic; add a piece of provolone cheese and a side of fresh vegetables and the simple meal was complete. The first course was always some pasta with butter or red sauce also combined with other vegetables laced with fresh garlic. The local town square markets sold fresh fish and meat.

Corleone is a hamlet located in a mountainous semi-arid region of Sicily made famous by the popular "Godfather" movie trilogy. The locals were suspicious of outsiders and clung to their own small group. Superstition and mistrust was common among the villagers and the Mafia held sway for many decades. Memories were long and if you received a favor from one of the Dons you were obligated to pay back in some form one day. If a family overstepped or didn't abide, vendettas were a common payback and payback could be serious business. The Mafia maintained control with fear and reprisals, even the Church did not stand in their way.

Corleone is off the beaten path and visitors had to have a reason to trudge up the dry rocky roads leading to the town square. Transportation was by horses or mules, pulling wagons or carts, and mostly merchants made the daily trip.

Sicily is strategically located off the toe of Italy, separated from it by the Strait of Messina, surrounded by the Mediterranean Sea. It looks like Italy is giving Sicily the boot!

In centuries past, Sicily was invaded and conquered by the Greeks, Moors and many other nations all claiming the right to call Sicily their own. They developed into a people of many ancestries and ethnic groups. Some were fair skinned with blue eyes, others darker skinned and Middle Eastern looking. Inter-marriage with conquering marauding nations created multi-cultural people who considered themselves special, shrewd and wise.

Like most Mediterranean cultures, the Sicilians were family and tradition oriented. They were under Roman Catholic authority and adhered to the strict doctrine of the Church.

These close-knit communities, with extended family all around, knew everyone else's business. Neighbors could be harshly judged and shunned for not complying with accepted traditions of the day.

Packing up and leaving home must have been a difficult decision for the many émigrés. They boarded a ship in Palermo with all the belongings they could reasonably carry and made the 30-day journey across the Atlantic. The conditions in steerage were unsanitary, crowded and lacked privacy. Some pregnant woman gave birth during the journey under those stressful and filthy conditions. Quite a few passengers became ill with dysentery, smallpox and other easily communicable diseases. Those who survived were stronger and had immune systems able to deal with these diseases. The hardships they suffered during the trip for them was well worth the freedom and opportunities they believed lay ahead.

The last day of the journey must have been spectacular for the many desperate travelers. They steamed into the wide New York harbor to be greeted by a tall verdigris statue, namely, the Statue of Liberty. Although worn to the bone, they must have experienced an exhilaration to have reached the American shores, where the "streets were paved with gold." After being processed through Ellis Island, most of the immigrants had family or a padrone (sponsor) to greet them. However, if they showed signs of illness, they were detained and quarantined on Ellis Island until they recovered.

The history of immigration in the US reveals many changes over the years and for many reasons. The laws shift to favor one ethnic group over another; once again, prejudice plays a big part in the process. It's quite complicated and evolving to the present day.

Grandpa Alfonso Lancona

Records show that Grandpa Al was born in the US in New York City. At some point he went to Italy and studied at a University in Naples where he obtained a degree in accounting. He was a whiz with figures and had a good business sense as well. Some stories told how he was an ardent student burying his head in books and was not a partier, a rather stern young man, and focused on his studies, not given to youthful distractions. Other details about his education are sketchy.

Grandpa Al returned to the US fortified with a college education. In September, 1908, he met Carmela Ferrara and they married. Soon a family was on the horizon, they had four children, Rose, Gerald, Salvatore and Maria. They purchased a home on Staten Island where the family grew and lived for many years, according to the census records of 1920, 1930 and 1940. During those years he obtained the position of Vice President of a local bank and did the books for a few private businesses.

Although the Lancona family went through the depression in the 1930's they didn't experience the deprived state that many others found themselves, although there was food rationing. Perhaps Grandpa Alfonso had some connections through friends or possibly the Masons. He was a long standing member of the brotherhood and he attained the level of 32nd degree Mason before he died in 1944.

Grandma did not reveal very much about her husband; although whatever was said described him as an upstanding man with good principles. His business dealings were private and not shared with the rest of the family. In those days being "head of the household" meant that his business and transactions were withheld from Grandma Carmela and the children. He provided a comfortable lifestyle.

During his career, he bought and sold real estate, owned a coffee shop, and did accounting for a couple of firms. As far as Grandma Carmela was concerned, he was an honorable man. They lived in the house at 86 Van Pelt Avenue, Staten Island about 30 years before moving to the small rent controlled apartment in the Bronx. It was supposed to be a temporary move, transitioning to another house north of the Woodlawn Cemetery on the Yonkers border. He was negotiating the purchase of a 6-story apartment building on DeKalb Avenue in the Bronx, near the apartment. These negotiations fell apart when Grandpa suddenly died of a massive heart attack at about the age of 56. Grandma and the children were totally ignorant about how to conduct business and pick up where Grandpa left off.

He left a substantial sum in a savings account and Grandma also had his social security. The stewardship of the monies was turned over to Uncle Jerry, since he was the oldest son. Over a short period of time the monies quickly were diminished through excessive and unnecessary spending on the part of the two brothers. According to tradition, the oldest son would be responsible for taking care of the widowed mother and sister.

That pretty much ended the future hopes and dreams of Marie, Grandma and Jonna.

Anything Goes

In the 1930's the American songwriter and composer Cole Porter, published a tune entitled "Anything Goes." The time period was after the first World War and in the 1920's when the younger generation wanted to break loose and get away from anything old fashioned or traditional. The "Roaring Twenties" brought styles of clothing and music that reflected a rebellious mindset as the skirts became shorter, the shorter hair styles were called bobs, the music got jazzier, and bootleg hooch flowed freely in the "Speak Easies." They danced to the Charleston, a type of energetic dance, revealing more leg and skin year by year. Famous movie stars like Jean Harlow sported the latest revealing fashion and hair styles as the masses of moviegoers ogled these gorgeous women and handsome men. "Talkies" and musicals began to pop up monthly as audiences ate up the genre. Before the 20's, silent movies were all that was available. Within a few relatively years the Victorian Age had vanished.

So Cole Porter wrote:

> *In oldern days a glimpse of stocking was looked on*
> *as something hocking, now heaven knows,*
> *Anything Goes!*
>
> *Good Authors too who once knew better words*
> *now only use four letter words writing pros,*

Anything Goes!

The world has gone mad today, and good's bad today and black's white today, and day's night today, when most guys today, that women prize today are just silly gigolos.

So though I'm not a great romancer I know that you are bound to answer when I propose.... Cause anything goes.

When Grandma Carmela arrived in the late 1800's and well into the 1900's she dressed in long skirts or dresses with long sleeves, laced up shoes, stockings, bloomers, corsets, gloves, hats and umbrellas to shield their skin from the sun. Most of the body was concealed. The summers must have been brutal! It must have taken an hour just to get dressed!

Some women used loose powder and rouge to pink up their cheeks. Make-up was mostly reserved for show-business people who were considered immodest and immoral. They probably dressed in revealing clothing, showing ankle and low cut blouses revealing bosoms.

New Yorkers traveled by trolly car; horse and carriage was reserved for the upper crust or shall we say the wealthy. The streets bustled with push carts and in some places gas lights were still operational. The gas lamps were lit at sundown by a "Lamplighter" and extinguished at sun up. Electric service was not always available. The streets were kept clean by "Sweeps;" they traveled the neighborhoods to collect not only trash, but horse pucky too!

A generation, by some, is counted every 10 years. The 1930's, 40's 50's and 60's would introduce revolutionary, (some might call progressive), attitudes in the modern world. The industrial age that began in the 1850's in Europe offered mass manufacturing and the so-called modern conveniences produced would lighten the workload for the average person, making life easier. The flip side was that many skilled laborers were displaced by machinery and unemployed.

In the 1940's many young men served in the military during World War II. Women became a strong presence in the workforce. Rosie-the-Riveter, became an icon for the working women of the nation!

The 1950's in some ways seemed more stable as returning soldiers regrouped, bought houses under the GI Bill and started families. Their children are known as "the baby boomers" those born after 1946 through 1964.

It's probably impossible for the young generation of the 21st century to comprehend the amazing world-wide changes in attitude, communication, social mores, over the past century. The young believe they know it all, believe that their knowledge and attitudes are progressive, they believe the world is their oyster, and that they can improve on the old and bring in the new.

I beg to remind that the expression "been there, done that" is reserved for those who have lived a full life of many years. They experienced one to one relationships, in person, face to face, without the aid of the internet or social media.

Perhaps the joys of a less cluttered and confusing lifestyle might become popular again......

The Depression

Grandma told Jonna lots of stories and some were of "The Great Depression" of the 1930's.

Note: The Great Depression was a severe worldwide economic depression that took place mostly during the 1930's beginning in the United States. The timing varied across the world; in most countries it started in 1929 and lasted until the late 1930's. The worldwide Great Depression is commonly used as an example of how intensely the global economy can decline.

The Lancona family didn't feel the effects of the depression as many others might have. Even with food shortages and rationing during those years, Grandpa Al continued to provide a comfortable lifestyle. However, most sectors of the economy were devastated, and, in general, the population suffered deprivation. There were limits of how much sugar, butter, gasoline and other essentials that could be purchased. Those were the years leading up to the start of World War II when citizens were asked to give up even more of their regular purchases.

It was also a time when those with "disposable income" were able to purchase tracks of foreclosed and abandoned properties and businesses. The poor became very poor and in some cases the moderately rich became extremely wealthy in the years following the war.

Jonna had no idea about how her family managed to survive relatively unscathed during those years. Grandma didn't elaborate. Grandpa Al's business connections and friends may have been a factor. Or that he was a 32nd degree Mason and had associates in high places. In reality, Jonna would never know.

Early 1940's

The coffee shop was a typical 1940's style diner nestled between the corner candy store and the Shamrock Bar. There was no table seating, only a long counter with red vinyl covered stools. They offered regular breakfast and lunch fare. It was a bustling establishment where locals and commuters regularly gathered for coffee and a donut, local news and gossip was freely shared and it became a sort of hang out for many.

Marie was 17-20 years old during those almost carefree days while Grandpa Alfonso was still alive. The Lancona siblings were pretty spoiled and lived the good life with plenty of everything.

Marie was a music fan. The big bands in the 1940's ushered in the "swing" generation. Benny Goodman, the Dorsey Brothers, Glen Miller and others fed a generation of fans that rivaled the Beatles of the 1960's. Bobby soxers swooned over Frank Sinatra and jitterbugged to the energetic sounds broadcast on every radio station. Radio and newspapers were the conduit for most of the music and information, along with 78 record discs.

Jonna's mother, Marie, was beautiful, talented and well positioned in life that offered her many freedoms. She had a good popular singing voice and aspired to be the female singer with the big bands. Weekly she would venture into the city and hang out backstage with a band, especially the

Benny Goodman Band. She was offered the opportunity to cut an audition record, which was well received by Benny himself. In those days, women who were considered for the singing spot had to do more than sing. The bandleaders wanted much more in the way of sexual favors, common in the entertainment field. Marie couldn't go along, or so the story goes, and didn't pursue the field much longer.

However, she loved the music and regularly attended night clubs and concerts offering the big band entertainment. She recalled going to the Paramount Theater in the city to see Frank Sinatra perform with the bands. She said the whole theater vibrated with sound, with the audience dancing in the aisles. What a time that must have been!

Often times Aunt Marge joined Marie, acting as chaperone, since she was quite young. The stories went on and on and Jonna felt the aura of some special and good times.

When Jonna came along, Marie was determined that she introduce her only child into show business in some form. She was being groomed to fit into that life. It didn't take..... but that's for a later chapter.

Lancona Phoenicia Vacations
The early days

Phoenicia was supposedly named after an Indian tribe that lived in the Catskill area a century or more before. The Esopus Creek, also an Indian name, meandered through the town and allowed for kayaking, tubing and other such romping and splashing about in the refreshing river water. The tributary reached high water in the spring as the snow melt cascaded downstream. Some of the locals dammed up the creek to form swimming holes; the water was fresh and cold all year long. It eventually spilled into the Aqueduct that ran from upstate New York all the way down to the city, going underground for a portion under the Hudson River. It was known as the Croton Aqueduct. Big sections had walking paths from Croton Dam, in Croton, NY, all the way down to Yonkers and the Henry Hudson Bridge connecting Bronx to Manhattan.

The Lancona's took regular summer vacations in Phoenicia staying at The Grand Phoenicia Hotel off of route 28. Marie accompanied Grandpa Al and Grandma Carmela for this annual summer pilgrimage to the country. Sometimes Uncle Sam, Uncle Jerry and Aunt Marge and Cousin Bea would come up for part of the time.

During one of the regular summer visits, Marie met Art Short; he was a local business owner operating a well-established dairy right in town. Marie was in her late teens and was given permission to date Art. Fathers had to give permission in those days and he was strict about who Marie associated with or dated in modern terminology. It was also called courting with honorable intentions. Art was well liked by the whole family and he and Marie kept up an on-and-off friendship for many years. Casual un-chaperoned dating was frowned upon then, so Art dated Marie with strict guidelines.

Those were wonderful carefree times spent in the Catskill Mountains. The family visited the surrounding towns; Hunter Mountain was one of the famous winter ski slopes in the area. The strong German influence was noticeable with the Chalet style architecture of the homes and the restaurants offering the best corned beef, wienerschnitzel and other typical German fare.

Fall and early winter brought hunters to that area of the Catskills and the local towns bustled with visitors all year long; it was a nearby destination for many city dwellers as well. The hunting season began in around mid-October; first for bow and arrow and then rifles; the Catskills were flooded with camouflage clad weekend warriors in search of deer buck for butchering and trophy collecting. Antlers or racks were prized, especially those with 7-10 points, whatever that meant.

The tradition of annual vacationing in the Phoenicia area was kept up by the siblings and their children for many years to come.

More about that later.

Pierre

Over the past several years Jonna has used the Ancestry.com program to obtain information about the family and along with Marie's input been able to arrange a sketchy composite of Pierre's life.

About 18 years ago, as of this writing, she was summoned to France to settle the estate of her deceased father, Pierre, and found quite a bit of information about his life archived in his villa flat. It seems like the Banderet's kept records dating from the early 1930's until the present, along with documents, photos, letters and miscellaneous correspondence. It took a bit of investigating to come up with a picture of events in his life leading up to the time he came to New York in 1941 since everything was written in French.

The records indicate that he was a merchant marine for the Swiss Army, traveling to many ports of call. He was a skilled mechanic and served aboard the ships in that capacity. Jonna found out that Pierre was born in Switzerland, ergo he was able to join the Swiss Army. The ancestry records show his departure and arrival on various vessels during the period of 1941 through approximately 1946.

Although he lived in France, in the hamlet of Beaulieu sur mer on the coast of the Mediterranean Sea, he was either drafted or enlisted in the Swiss Navy. The Second World War was raging in Europe and Hitler was invading France and occupying many cities in the North around Paris. The underground was active and pressed on all sides in the conflict. Very difficult times for the French people as neighbor turned against neighbor, food was scarce; fear and isolation and distrust became the order of the day. Families were devastated. Perhaps the southern coastal towns like Nice, Cannes and Beaulieu sur mer didn't feel the impact as strongly as the Parisians. However, their country was under attack and all citizens felt the repercussions.

Jonna's French/Swiss grandparents owned and operated a hotel in Cannes and an antique business on the ground floor of the building. They purchased a villa with several flats where they lived in one of them and rented out the others to extended family. There were gardens around the villa with lemon and other citrus trees that thrived in the micro climate of the region. Pierre was an only child and received the full attention and doting from wealthy parents. Life was good. Many of the town's residents swam in the waters of the Mediterranean from the beaches next to the marina. There were medium to small yachts moored there, and upscale shops lined the waterfront walkway; this was the French Riviera after all!

It is unclear how Peter, as he was called in the US, entered the country. It is believed that he was aboard a ship that docked in New York Harbor. He may have been on shore leave, left the ship and never returned. Once again sketchy stories do not tell the whole tale.

Nevertheless, he fell in love with the city and made his way through the borough of Manhattan to the Bronx. Here is where the story begins to take some shape as far as Jonna is concerned.

Marie and Peter

They both came from moderately wealthy families whose protection shielded them from some of the realities of life. Jonna came to understand that the attractive couple were far from ready to marry and become parents.

Peter stepped off on the subway platform at the 206th street exit, the end of the line on that route. He climbed the grimy subway steps and was greeted by the steam fogged windows of the coffee shop. It seemed welcoming; he took a seat at the counter and ordered an American coffee. Marie was behind the counter when their eyes met.

Peter spoke little English and Marie no French. Introductions and some halted conversation ensued. Everyone in the shop was interested in the young handsome seaman who regaled them with stories of his homeland. Some stories seemed unbelievable; after all why was he away from the wonderful surroundings in the south of France and how did he wind up in the Bronx?

The attraction grew as Marie and Peter began seeing one another away from the coffee shop. Grandpa Al's antennae were tweaking as he observed the relationship becoming serious. Peter was not to his liking, he was a young foreigner with no occupation and in the Navy. But like all wise fathers he understood that his interference would be unwelcomed and he would look like the bad guy if he came down hard on the relationship.

On that note, when he realized that they were not to be put off, he insisted that they marry so as to avoid premarital sexual relations and God forbid, pregnancy. It was only a few months after Peter entered the coffee shop when the infatuated couple headed downtown into the city and were married. They tied the knot on Saturday, October 31st, 1942. The service was conducted by Lawrence B. Larson, Rector at the Church of the Holy Nativity. Aunt Marge and Uncle Sam were the witnesses. Both Peter and Marie were 20 years old.

At first they lived in the apartment with Grandma Carmela and Grandpa Al, but that lasted a short time. Eventually they took a room in a boarding house on Bainbridge Avenue, just a few blocks away from the coffee shop and the apartment on Rochambeau Avenue.

The dynamics of their life together took many turns. Mostly, according to Marie, there was discord, stress and all around dissatisfaction within the marriage. There was abuse, both physical and emotional. Not to put a fine point on it, it was a disaster.

Marie became pregnant just 3 months after the wedding. Jonna arrived on November 9th in 1943. She was Christened Jeanne-Marie Leoni Carmela Banderet a couple of months later. The Leoni name, was after her French Grandmother, and Carmela after Marie's Sicilian mother.

With stressors coming from all directions, Marie's life was in trouble. The next several years would prove to be devastating for her. Some of the scenarios are forthcoming in the next few chapters.

California

During one of Peter's return visits to the US, he secured a job that involved a move to California, in Beverly Hills. Through some unknown connections, the DeVeilliers offered Peter and Marie jobs with Jonna in tow. These folks were movie moguls and lived in the nearby suburbs of Beverly Hills, the heart of the movie making industry. The family of three would be provided an over-the-garage apartment. Peter would be chauffeur and mechanic in charge of keeping the Benz spit and polish clean. Marie was part-time housekeeper. There were other employees on staff, so the job did not at first seem overly burdensome.

The new destination and experience was probably supposed to give the couple a fresh start away from family. Maybe they thought that the marriage would improve.

They drove a bulky Packard automobile that was provided by the DeVeilliers out of New York, down the Pennsylvania Turnpike and other connecting secondary state roads to Chicago where they picked up Route 66 toward St. Louis. After crossing the Mississippi River the great frontier lay before them. The interstate travel system had not yet been established. There were services along the way for food, fuel, stands with local crafts, fresh produce and lodging, historical markers and sightseeing detours.

The trip was an adventure of a lifetime for Marie. She marveled at the vast plains, desert expanse, rocky outcroppings and majestic sunsets. The Indian wares she purchased along the way were made of sterling silver and turquoise fashioned into typical Native American jewelry. Marie wanted to take pictures, but one Indian said "me brakum camera." She decided that maybe picture taking was not such a good idea. They entered California through the town of Needles on the Arizona border.

The year was 1948 or 1949 and Jonna was about 5-6 years old. She didn't remember the trip. Photos were the only triggers and, of course, Marie's recollections. California felt like paradise: the balmy, sunny weather, where palm trees, orange and other fruit trees grew freely along the streets and boulevards. It was a stark contrast compared to the Bronx with hot, humid summers and gloomy overcast winters. California offered the feeling of a carefree abundant lifestyle.

But it was not to be, possibly because Marie did not like the feeling of being a household servant. Or maybe because she missed the family connection back east. Whatever the reason, the Banderet's were soon packed up, without a car, and boarded an eastbound Santa Fe train, leaving paradise and heading home to New York. The city may not have been warm and fuzzy, but it was home and close to family once again.

Intervening Years

Between the time Jonna was born and the time she entered school in 1st grade, there were probably many disrupting events that took place. For the most part, Jonna does not recall anything like that.

One particular recurring memory was when she was on Ellis Island, seated on a wooden bench just outside a door; there was some kind of a meeting going on. Pierre was being processed to be deported back to France. He knelt down in front of Jonna and begged "tell your mother not to send me away."

During those years, Jonna received many lovely gifts from Grandpa Paul and Grandma Leoni. One Particular gift was a round gold pendant with Jeanne D'arc's image on one side with Jonna's initials and birthday on the other side; it was accompanied by an intricately weaved gold chain. Another gift was a small rounded edge sewing purse made of red snake skin; the sewing implements were made of ivory. Marie was given pure essence oil of Chanel #5 kept in the top dresser drawer for many years. These imports, among others, were of high quality and constructed with first-grade materials.

Marie was determined to keep distance between Jonna and her French grandparents. Letters were exchanged where they suggested that Marie and Jonna visit them in Nice. At that time Jonna was their only grandchild and they wanted her to experience the wonderful lifestyle on the Riviera and all the advantages and culture the wealthy grandparents could provide.

Marie was a burned and scorned woman with a Sicilian temper and vindictive attitude. She wanted to punish Pierre for all his misgivings. Jonna was caught in the crossfire and was deprived of knowing her French grandparents. In one of the correspondences, Marie accused Peter of "molesting" young Jonna. She was determined not to have a repeat performance and began the deportation proceedings. The grounds for this action also remain sketchy. This proved to be the ultimate punishment for Jonna's father; he feared returning to France for some unknown reason.

With the source of great stress removed, life began to look more normal. Marie was controlling her life now without interference. Control in the name of love was her MO. Although Jonna was pampered and fussed over she was also held on a tight leash; there were strict dos and don't's and boundaries which seemed normal at the time.

The following years Marie took up Bible study under the tutelage of the Watchtower Bible and Tract Society ie, Jehovah's Witnesses. Jonna remembers Marie poring over thick volumes published by the Society until all hours of the night; it was a training manual the missionaries completed before receiving their assignments. It amounted to about a six-month course.

Perhaps Marie needed a strong discipline to fill the gaps in her life and provide answers that she was looking for. Maybe that would be the saving grace for her in the light of the previous 10 years of anxiety and stress.

Grandma Carmela, 1939 World's Fair.

Marie, early 1940's. Grandpa Al's car.

Baby Jonna with Uncle Sam.

Uncle Sam and Jonna in stroller, circa 1944.

Part II

The Witnesses

In or around the year 1945 Grandma Carmela answered a knock on the door and greeted a man and a woman calling themselves "Bible Students." They seemed like a nice couple and offered to conduct a free home Bible study at Grandma's convenience. She asked a few questions, liked their responses and agreed to the study.

Previously and for many years, Grandma was a Bible reader. She had lots of questions. She approached a local priest and asked him to explain some scriptures and passages. He told her that some things in the Bible were unexplained and remained a mystery and best left unquestioned. Gradually she began to shy away from the Catholic Church, which opened the door for the Bible Students to begin a study.

Grandma liked the Bible study and was satisfied with the explanations given by the Bible teachers. The dogma of the Catholic Church seemed way out of line and many of the practices unnecessary. The Bible students explained that many of the icons, rituals and practices of the Church were rooted in paganism and idolatry; the simple teaching of the Messiah, and later the Apostles, was not reflected in the Church. Over the centuries, the Church evolved away from a pure worship of God and His son Christ Jesus.

Marie tuned in to the Bible study and was equally pleased with the teaching. Soon the Banderet/Lancona household hosted a weekly "book study" group at the apartment that was held on a Tuesday evening, starting at 7:00 pm and ending at 8:00 pm. The study for each new publication was completed in about six months. Marie and Jonna read the assigned chapter, and underlined the answers to the questions. Brother Petros, an older Greek man, conducted the study and welcomed Jonna's simple answers. She was sometimes asked to read a Bible passage suggested in the book.

There were usually six brothers and sisters in attendance, in addition to the conductor, Grandma, Marie and Jonna. The local Kingdom Hall loaned the household some folding wooden chairs to accommodate with the seating. Around this time, the Bible students were renamed "Jehovah's Witnesses."

Grandma and Marie subscribed to the weekly publication called The Watchtower with its accompanying magazine called Awake. They pored over these magazines and Grandma began to copy the journals, in flourishing script handwriting, into school notebooks. After a few years, these notebooks were collected together and stacked in the back bedroom to over four feet tall!

The Society, meaning, The Watchtower Bible and Tract Society, strongly encouraged attendance to the Sunday meeting held at the Kingdom Hall; the nearest Hall was located at 182nd Street and Third Avenue in the Bronx. Marie took Jonna to these meetings fairly regularly for a while. Jonna only remembers having to sit absolutely still with her hands folded in her lap, for the duration of the public talk and Watchtower study.

Although meeting attendance became infrequent, Marie prepared lessons that Jonna completed after school. On her own, Jonna loved reading excerpts from the book of Proverbs, Ecclesiastes and Matthew especially the passages called The Sermon on the Mount.

The organization told the new Witnesses that they were required to preach the Good News or Gospel from door to door, as was done in the days of the Apostles. This did not go over well with Grandma. Instead of meeting with the group to go "door to door" she conducted a Bible study with a woman in the neighborhood.

Grandma and Mrs. Reina, shared a common background; both were immigrants from the town of Corleone, Sicily. Mrs. Reina could not read or write and welcomed Senora Lancona into her home to read and explain the Bible. Jonna often accompanied Grandma on these visits. The two old ladies drank Bustello brand espresso coffee and Jonna dunked biscotti and sesame seed cookies in her milk.

A side note:

The Reina family lived in a 3-story old style stucco house with a fenced in garden and grounds that rested in the shadow of Jonna's building. There was a shallow rectangle pool on the grounds that housed big goldfish at one time.

Fronting the house was a long set of concrete stairs sided by pillars topped with lions heads. This may have been symbolic representing the town of Corleone, meaning heart of a lion.

All along Rochambeau Avenue houses with small back and front yards were interspersed among the apartment buildings. Some had professional offices, others private residences.

Mrs. Reina, already a widow of almost 20 years, was a stay-at-home old fashioned woman. She cooked and cleaned for her large family of 6; three boys and three girls. Millie, her oldest daughter did most of the shopping. Marie and Uncle Sam hung out with her children during holidays and Italian feast days.

Unbeknownst to everyone in the neighborhood, Mrs. Reina's husband, Gaetano, was one of the Capos in La Cosa Nostra, which when roughly translated means Our thing. He was killed by a shotgun head wound at the age of 40; he died instantly. He had a history of gang related activity and became a member of the "Lucchese" crime family. By the year 1920 Reina had formed his own family and controlled criminal operations in The Bronx and parts of East Harlem. Gaetano Reina was laid to rest in the famous Woodlawn Cemetery in the Bronx.

There were mostly 2nd generation Jewish immigrants in the neighborhood around Rochambeau Avenue. They had no idea that such activities were conducted right under their noses, so to speak. It was kept quiet, for the most part, until the book "The Valachi Papers" was published in 1972, where most of the Mafia and crime family connections were clearly revealed. Valachi was Reina's son-in-law married to Millie Reina. It was at that time that his connection to organized crime became known. He spilled the beans to the FBI and supposedly received a lighter sentence after being convicted. The book was a pretty big seller in the New York area.

Telephones and TV's

These were simpler times.

Jonna's earliest memory of a telephone was a desk model black rotary dial phone with a cloth covered cable. It was heavy and clunky. Oftentimes these phones sat on a special telephone table with an adjoining seat and a shelf for the thick telephone directory books for your area.

At that time, circa 1952, there were no area codes and telephone exchanges had name prefixes, for example, OLinville was OL5-9251 a Bronx exchange for the location around Mosholu Parkway and Bainbridge Avenue. Another was Murray Hill, an upper east-side of Manhattan exchange, mentioned in the I Love Lucy episodes. The famous book and movie "Butterfield 8" written by John O'Hara defined the silk stocking district in NYC. Others were Canal, KNickerbocker, PEnnsylvania (made famous in Glen Miller's rendition of the 1930's tune Pennsylvania 6-5000, which by the way, has been in continuous use to the present day. GEdney (Brooklyn) NEptune (Queens) GReenleaf (Scarsdale) GIbralter and STgeorge for Staten Island. Both of Grandma's sisters Aunt Mary and Aunt Rose had GIbralter exchanges. The telephone had an ear-piercing ring that couldn't be adjusted. There were no "while you were away messaging" or "call waiting" features. If you missed a call, the caller tried again later. If someone was already talking on the dialed number, you got a busy signal and had to try your call again later. The Lancona/Banderet household used the telephone infrequently, as the circle of family contacts were limited. When calling a doctor or other service provider, there was a live person or secretary to answer your call. There was no music or other announcements while waiting to talk to your party. There were no menus or choices, which seems awful primitive in these modern times!

These were more personal times

To get information, you dialed "0" on the rotary. A live operator would get you the number. If there were a few names alike, you might have to supply a street address to clarify. It was not possible to dial long-distance direct, once again an operator would place the call for you; an additional charge would appear on your next phone bill. Later these would be called toll calls. There even was a service announcing the time and date! Some people chose to have their number unlisted and not available for disclosure by the operator. For an emergency, or to report something, you contacted your local precinct to speak with a desk sergeant who took down the information and dispatched a police car to the area. The 52nd precinct served the area for Jonna's neighborhood. Montefiori Hospital was located at the end of Rochambeau Avenue bordered by Gun Hill Road on the north side. The hospital was within a short walking distance from Jonna's apartment, easily accessible in an emergency.

These were less politically correct times

There were no options for hearing or visually impaired callers. Back in that day, people who were sight-impaired were called blind; folks with hearing disabilities were called deaf. People who had trouble walking were called crippled. There were no handicap parking spaces; sidewalks didn't have ramps to the street or automatic door openers. Euphemisms were inserted in the language many years later as politically correct expressions worked their way into the vocabulary.

These were times of unsophisticated entertainment.

They got their first tv in 1951 when Jonna was about 8 years old. It had a 10" screen (measured on the diagonal) surrounded by greyish-brown boxy wood cube. The back could be removed and tubes replaced when they burned out. Sprouting from the top rear were two retractable metal antennae for reception, referred to as rabbit ears. If reception wasn't good, as often was the case, they would affix tinfoil flags to the antennae or stuck the hook end of a wire clothes hanger in the slot. This sometimes worked.

All TVs at that time were broadcast in black and white. Channel 2, 4, and 7, i.e, CBS, NBC and ABC respectively. Popular shows like I Love Lucy, the Ed Sullivan Show, the Dinah Shore show and others aired weekly with singers and dancers and comedy skits. Edward R. Murrow hosted the regular news broadcasts at 6:00 pm and 11:00 pm. Saturday mornings were for the kids. Shows like Howdy Doody, Mickey Mouse cartoons and Hop-along Cassidy westerns and don't forget the Lone Ranger and Tonto his faithful sidekick.

The soap operas were shown from noon to 4:00 in the afternoon. Shows like General Hospital, The Days of our Lives and The Guiding Light. These shows were called "soaps" because detergent and other household cleaners were advertised, appealing to the female stay-at-home audiences of the 1950's. The channels were manually changed, brightness and volume adjusted by rotating the dials.

After the 11:00 p.m. nightly news went off the air, the Star-Spangled Banner was played immediately followed by a test pattern, which was a circular emblem that dominated the screen. An emergency siren would blast for a few seconds and that officially ended the broadcasts. That would disappear too followed by snow like white specks dancing around.

And even after those dancing white specks, some would watch the screen for a while longer. I guess folks at that time were more easily entertained.

A new product came on the market called tv dinners, a frozen dinner, usually white and dark meat turkey with mashed potatoes and green beans or meatloaf with mashed potatoes and green peas; lots of brown gravy made them somewhat palatable. The brand name Swanson hit the tv viewing audiences by storm and families were pictured eating these dinners in front of the tv… on newly invented tv trays that were folded and stacked and put away. These simple dinners were housed in a tinfoil type of tray, to be heated in the oven for 25 minutes; microwaves were not available.

The Lancona family gave these dinners a try, but were swiftly rejected because they tasted bland, using instant mashed potatoes and overcooked vegetables. They felt that you either ate dinner at a table or watched tv. Doing both at the same time was unacceptable.

During those years, the producers adhered to strict guidelines about the content of the broadcasts. The use of curse words was out of the question and sexual content cleverly disguised. Even Lucy and Ricky slept in separate beds although they were a married couple. How archaic was that!

The years following the widespread availability of tv shows showed galloping advancement in technology. Color TVs became affordable and the shows presented grew in sophistication and stage sets became more elaborate.

When the household went quiet, Jonna would quietly find a channel that showed the very old movies produced in the late 1930's and early 1940's. Movies like Charlie Chan (a Chinese detective and his sidekick son) The Werewolf, starring Lon Chaney Jr., the Mummy starring Boris Karloff, Sherlock Holmes starring Basil Rathbone and his medical associate Dr. Watson, The Hunchback of Notre Dame, starring Maureen O'Hara and Charles Laughton, written by Victor Hugo, to name but a few. Oh yes, there was Frankenstein starring Boris Karloff and the Vampire starring Bela Lugosi. Jonna would be engrossed with the films until late at night. These movies were not technically advanced, but were very suspenseful in Jonna's eyes. The movie sets were simple and unsophisticated, but movie goers of the day seemed contented enough and entertained nonetheless.

Rag Pickers and Fish Mongers

Every other week on a Friday, the jingling of the fish monger would herald his presence in the neighborhood. He arrived in a horse-drawn wagon loaded down with all sorts of fresh fish, the day's catch, brought up from Fulton Fish Market in lower Manhattan. Grandma Carmela gave Jonna a few dollars to purchase a pound of flounder filet. The fish would be breaded and fried in butter served along with mashed potatoes made from scratch. They used a hand held masher implement to smooth out the lumpy potatoes. Jonna got very good at this mashing, adding lots of butter and warm milk, salt and pepper, just before dinner was served. Yummy!

Once a month, the rag pickers made the rounds, up and down the neighborhood streets, also in a horse-drawn wagon shouting what sounded like "I cash clothes" as they slowly passed the buildings. Residents brought down their old, ready to be discarded clothing in exchange for a few pennies on the pound. The old clothing was again sold, some repaired, others distributed for the needy. Most of the rag pickers were headquartered in and around Hester Street in the city, where mostly Jewish clothing merchants imported and resold a wide range of apparel.

These horse-drawn wagons were soon to be replaced with gasoline powered trucks that resembled open sided push carts. Once again these services dwindled in the early 1950's. They became relics of a by-gone era.

One service that continued into the mid 1950's was door delivery of dairy products, bread, soft drinks, seltzer and even bleach water. Grandma called the bleach Chavella water. Jonna had no idea where that name came from. A wooden box held the day's delivery with a note attached listing the reorder. Every product was available in glass, reusable containers only. Plastic coated containers, plastic wrap of any sort, came into use a bit later, which led to more garbage to be burned. Most cold cuts and sliced cheeses were wrapped in wax paper or shiny butcher paper. Butter was cut from a large oblong slab and portioned out by the grocer. Groceries were put in paper bags. Big head, as Marie coined the local grocer, used a black crayon type of pencil to mark the cost of the items on the bag; he quickly added up the purchases without the use of a calculator; he was never off even by a penny.

The streets were swept about once a week by a city worker pushing a galvanized garbage can on wheels. When alternate side of the street parking came into effect, his employment ended and was replaced by garbage trucks with swirling circular brooms. Another job lost for unskilled workers.

Products, like paper towels, wipes, Pampers and Huggies were not yet available for general use or polyester and synthetic blended fabrics as well. However, nylon stockings were still in fashion; cotton cloths were used and reused and washed until they were threadbare and full of holes; there wasn't much waste. The term, recycling came into use many years later in or around the 1980's when formal recycling procedures became more common.

The Neighborhood

The neighborhood where Jonna grew up in was actually 3 neighborhoods bordering and overlapping one another. Those who rented apartments on Rochambeau Avenue, Mosholu Parkway and up to the Grand Concourse were mostly 2nd generation Jews. Their parents and grandparents were those who may have survived the Holocaust or escaped before the Jews were rounded up and sent to "work camps" awaiting execution in the gas chambers. After years living in the Ghetto on the lower east side of Manhattan, many made another exodus to the suburbs of the Bronx where it seemed countrified with local tree-lined parks, parkways and byways and green space.

The pre-war buildings were very attractive (buildings built between 1900 and 1939) and offered comfortable living space in relatively safe neighborhoods. Along the Grand Concourse some of the apartment buildings had canopies along with a liveried doorman to allow entrance. Some sections of the Concourse had a tree-lined island down the center separating the lanes.

Bainbridge Avenue ran north and south and curved around from Gun Hill Road on the north side and terminated at Webster Avenue on the south. On the east side of Bainbridge Avenue folks of Irish ancestry dominated the apartment buildings and many attended St. Brenan's

Church and school. Some of the children went to PS 80, the neighborhood public school that Jonna also attended. The Shamrock Bar and Grill was the local watering hole; it had a pleasant smell of beer and Irish pub fare wafting out the doors.

On the far side of the Grand Concourse was Villa Avenue where many immigrant Italians and their children lived. Their neighborhood had a few stores and some single family row type houses interspersed with apartment buildings. On the 4th of July, the residents made a big show with fireworks and all kinds of loud incendiary explosives that were heard for blocks around, even up to Rochambeau Avenue. Jonna was allowed to have sparklers and punks as the evening drew close to dark. They didn't make that much of the 4th on Rochambeau Avenue. Some kids had fire crackers and small rockets that were launched in the school yard.

There was almost everything you needed available along Bainbridge Avenue and the intersecting side streets. These businesses and shops catered to a wide variety of ethnic groups such as Germans and Poles along with the Jews, Irish and Italians. While Grandma was still able, Jonna would accompany Gram and help her with the shopping. Some of the merchants had their wares on shelves outside the store; like the fruit and vegetable market and sometimes the hardware store.

Most of the local residents frequented these stores for all their shopping. The only supermarket was down on Bainbridge Ave toward Webster Ave. It was called the A&P, the letters stood for Atlantic and Pacific Tea Company. The merchants and services along the way included a Chinese laundry, dress shops that carried a variety of women's apparel, a couple of grocery stores, a luncheonette, a hobby shop, The Bainbridge Movie Theater, a public library, a deli, meat market, a pizzeria, a couple of pubs and a few candy stores with luncheonettes.

On the corner of 206th St and Bainbridge Avenue, stood Lessel's Drug

Store; the Pharmacy filled prescriptions and offered a variety of goods and goodies you might expect to find in any modern day pharmacy section of the superstores. Most of the merchants recognized the local patrons and called them by name, which created a personal touch and a welcoming feeling with the shopping experience.

The luncheonette on the opposite corner from the pharmacy was bustling with customers picking up newspapers, magazines, cigarettes, bouncing pinkie Spalding balls, all kinds of candy and stationery supplies. It also had a soda fountain. Marie allowed Jonna to get an "egg cream," an exclusive Bronx creation consisting of chocolate syrup, milk and seltzer. No eggs! They also served sandwiches with the fixings. This particular candy store was bustling with morning commuters and the neighborhood kids after school; it was located just outside of the subway entrance.

After all is said, this neighborhood was a mixed community that provided most of the daily needs for their residents; everything was within a short walking distance and very convenient. "Blue laws" were still in effect and everything was closed on Sundays.

Note: The term "blue law" was first used back in 1755. It is legislation that prohibits or restricts certain activities in order to support religious standards. The Puritans were probably the first to enforce Sunday laws on the North American continent, banning many commercial and recreational activities on Sundays during the 1600s. Soon laws were added to prohibit the selling of alcoholic beverages on Sunday.

Arthur Avenue

About once a month, Grandma and Jonna boarded the local city bus and made the trip to Arthur Avenue, the "Little Italy" section of the Bronx intersected by 187th Street. Jonna found this very exciting: the neighborhood was full of different and interesting sights and smells.

They headed to the market. It was just called the market and offered many different stalls and vendors selling their wares. The floors of the aisles were painted grey. Along either side were vendors selling fruit, vegetables, juicy ripened figs, cheeses, meats, bread, cooking utensils, imported pasta, olive oil, olives of every variety, and canned tomatoes with basil among other canned and imported specialties.

The meat section displayed all sorts of exotic animal entrails, guts, stomachs, (also known as tripe), pigs feet, lamb heads, brains, (called cervelo), tongues, skinned rabbits, calves liver and other unfamiliar animal parts. Just looking at that display really grossed Jonna out. When Grandma was a young girl, she worked at a butcher shop for a while and learned about the select cuts of meat, and how to cut and trim the pieces. At the market, she purchased the fresh daily made sausage and thin cut meat for braciole. Just thinking about the sauce that would soon be simmering on the stove, with all these delicacies, along with fresh garlic and some onion was enough to stir her appetite. The fresh roma tomatoes were first blanched, peeled, and hand squeezed through a sieve, extracting the sweet thick juice and leaving behind the pulp and seeds.

After leaving the Market, they strolled along Arthur Avenue and perused the fresh fish displayed in wicker style baskets. Chipped ice covered the fish to keep it cold and fresh. One basket held small fish with big eyes; maybe they were sardines. Grandma occasionally purchase live snails to prepare for dinner. Although the garlic, olive oil and lemon and fresh parsley sauce was wonderful, Jonna didn't really like the chewy snails. However, coupled with a large slice of fresh bread, they were somewhat palatable. The escargot offered on the menu of high price restaurants were considered a delicacy, but the Lanconas had them pretty regularly; it was no big deal. A thin cut spaghetti (spaghettini #9) was a side dish along with some fresh greens to complete the meal. The next day, a couple of escaped snails were found attached to the side of the kitchen sink. Still alive!

Now let's talk about the deli section. Goodness gracious, that was the highlight of the shopping trip. Large provolone cheeses hanging from hooks, tied with twine and, dripping with oil, hung from the ceiling. Fresh daily made mozzarella and fresh grated pungent Locatelli cheese, prosciutto, hams, salami, were also purchased. These deli cuts are called "carne crudo" literally meaning raw meat. Olives of all descriptions were also displayed as well as imported vinegar and dried spices. The vendors called Grandma "signora" and offered samples for approval before wrapping up each purchase. Heavenly!

Down the street stood the corner game market; it was a small warehouse type building housing cages with chickens, rabbits, hens and other live game. It smelled awful in there and Jonna felt like gagging and throwing up. Grandma, undeterred by this reaction, ordered a chicken, which was subsequently slaughtered, plucked and placed in butcher paper with the giblets on the side in another wrapping. The roasted chicken with Grandma's special stuffing was prepared with mashed potatoes and a side of greens. Jonna was in charge of the mashies and loaded them with butter and warm milk. Very tasty indeed!

Grandma and Jonna made their way to the end of Arthur Avenue where Gram stopped for one last purchase. The shop was dark and smelled of pipe tobacco and cigarettes. The windows had advertisements for all sorts of brand name tobacco products that were available. Grandma discretely purchased some snuff, which she carried in a small tin. Snuff is a very finely ground tobacco, like a brown powder. The procedure was to use the index finger and thumb to pinch off a small bit to be inserted in the nostrils; a pinch for each side which sometimes caused sneezing; this habit was not to be advertised and Jonna was sworn to secrecy.

It was time to get back to their neighborhood on 206th Street. They boarded the bus, with purchases in tow, and headed home. The "vagela," a metal wagon with wheels, was loaded down to overflowing, a sumptuous dinner awaited.

These are some of the fondest memories in Jonna's young life and kept vivid by visits to Arthur Avenue over the years and into adulthood.

Music, music, music

"Put another nickel in, in the nickelodeon, all I want is loving you and music, music, music. I'd do anything for you, anything you want me to, all I want is kissing you and music, music, music." That recording by Theresa Brewer became a hit record in the early 1950's. She was an extremely popular recording artist and her records made the hit parade many times during her career.

For as long as Jonna can remember there was music in the home, either from the radio or 78 record discs played on the Grundig Majestic radio/turntable. The record player was housed in a fancy wood cabinet; the music came out sweet and clear.

One year Marie bought a red painted honky-tonk style piano; it was apartment sized and occupied a niche in the living room. Marie was talented and wrote a few songs, which she also played on the piano; one song was for Jonna, named "Keep Smiling For Me Please." She had a good ear for tunes and played relatively well for a novice. Jonna posed for a photo shoot on top of the piano along with other dance poses, some with pink ballet toe shoes on. Boy they hurt! Jonna had great respect for dancers who performed with the torturous footwear. She watched the movie "the Red Shoes" whenever it showed on tv; Moire Shearer starred in the famous ballet; she was mesmerized by the performance and story.

Along with the hit tunes of the day, Jonna was privileged to listen to very old recordings of the famous opera tenor, Enrico Caruso. Grandma, along with Grandpa Al, attended opera performances at the Met during the hey-day of opera in the 1920's and 30's. Carmela had recordings of opera singers like Amelita Galli Curci, who was a coloratura soprano and one of the most famous in her day. The record discs were large, 12 inches in diameter and very heavy; the turntable played records at speeds of 8 and 1/3, 16 and 2/3, 33 and 1/3, 45's, and 78's. Even on those old shellacked discs, the sound was majestic and thrilling. The expression "you sound like a broken record" was coined from when a needle skipped or jumped back to the previous groove due to a malfunction or scratch on the record. The expression "in the groove" probably came from the idea of being on track or "with it" as the hippies might say.

Carlo Buti was a popular singer in the 1930's who sang Neopolitan popular tunes; his voice was distinct and lively. Jonna remembers when Grandma purchased these records during one of their shopping trips to Arthur Avenue. Two of the recordings were "Vivere," meaning lively or full of life and "non dimenticar le mie parole," meaning don't forget my words. Jonna listened to these 78 records so many times that she was able to sing along with Carlo and mimicked his sound as she became attuned to Italian pronunciation and sound; Grandma also taught Jonna many short ditties in the language as well.

The record player played on and on with big band recordings, 1940's tunes, jazz and, of course... Frank Sinatra. The radio was her constant companion and Jonna absorbed these musical arrangements through her pores; she felt the music down to her bones.

By the mid-1950's, rock and roll dominated the air waves to the consternation of both Marie and Grandma. They thought that real music had gone the way of Balaam, substituted by the drone of repetitive doo wop and falsetto group street sounds. The dreamy romantic sounds were disappearing quickly, replaced by what Grandma called "noise." Elvis made his appearance on the world stage of entertainment and was one of the early pioneers of a blend of country and western and the softer rock and roll, laced with his own personal southern sound and style; the teenagers went crazy for the handsome fellow. The screaming and panting fans adored the new guy as his popularity grew far and wide to the greater world audiences.

While Jonna was not critical of the new music sound, she favored the mellower sounds and syncopated music of the 1940's. In reflection, Jonna noticed that each "generation" encompassing about a ten-year time frame, introduces a newer and different sound replacing the one before, and the cycle continues. Until the early 20th century, music appreciation was largely based on the classical compositions written a hundred years before. Before record distribution and player victrolas came into popular use, musical theaters, vaudeville acts and live club performances were the main sources for music entertainment.

Maybe the expression, "the more things change, the more they stay the same," has application, not only in the field of entertainment but in life in general. When everything old is new again!

The Holidays

One of the most puzzling aspects of being a JW was how the holidays were handled. According to the Witnesses, these religious and secular holidays were of dubious or pagan origin and not to be celebrated.

Grandma Carmela asserted that "for the sake of peace in the family," Marie and Jonna and herself would participate by attending these celebrations held at Aunt Marge and Uncle Jerry's house. They made a big deal out of the holidays and celebrated them to the hilt.

For instance, on Christmas Eve, Uncle Jerry hauled a 7' live pine tree, purchased at the local vegetable stand. The wonderfully smelling trees were displayed and stacked up on the sidewalk, loosely tied together with jute twine. The tree was secured atop his Cadillac sedan, and brought up in the elevator to the fifth floor and set-up in the corner of the living room. One of the kids had to retrace their steps and sweep up the dropped pine needles along the way.

A box holding the tree ornaments, bulbs, tinsel and other decorations was taken out of storage (beneath the bed) and neatly arranged below the tree. Tree decorating was taken very seriously. Jonna and Dennis had to be very careful with their assignment of putting the plastic icicles and tinsel neatly and symmetrically on the limbs. Uncle Jerry uttered some expletives when one of the bulbs in the string was not lighting. Each bulb had to be tested to find the burned-out one and replace it or the whole string of lights wouldn't light. Putting up the tree on Christmas Eve was an unbroken tradition for many years. Aunt Marge was busy in the kitchen preparing one of her sumptuous dinners of turkey with all the fixins, sweating over boiling and simmering pots.

After Dennis went to bed, the gifts were spread beneath the tree, indicating that Santa had left them for the recipients to be opened on Christmas Day. Dennis still believed in Santa and Jonna was sworn to be quiet about dispelling the myth. Aunt Marge took Bea and Gerald to midnight mass at St. Brendan's Church located on the other side of Bainbridge Avenue in the Irish section of the neighborhood.

Cousin Bea loved buying and wrapping presents. Sequestered in her bedroom, she busied herself with the annual project. Jonna felt a bit funny about receiving presents and not reciprocating. But she accepted the arrangement without complaint.

Christmas morning they all gathered around the tree for distribution of what Santa left for them. Uncle Jerry made it special by saying "good things come in small packages," or "ooo this one is heavy, I wonder what could be in this box." After handing out gifts it would soon be time to converge on the small dining area in the kitchen for a wonderful meal, everything made from scratch.

Grandma's tradition was to make a Sicilian bread called sfingiune. Jonna remembers the prep that began the preceding day. Grandma had a very large dough board brought out from the back of the kitchen closet for the occasion. Several cheeses were thinly sliced and piled high in dishes awaiting their distribution. Real sharp provolone, reggio parmigiana, mozzarella and to top it off several tins of anchovies in olive oil. The pots of rising dough were strewn across the counters and spilled into the warm living room; they were covered with a damp cloth to keep the moisture in.

After doubling in volume, the dough was punched down and permitted to rise again for another hour or so. Finally, the pans were fitted with the tender dough and layered with the cheeses and anchovies, a bit of olive oil, and some sprinkled oregano. There was enough to feed an army! And the smell of the baking delicacy made Jonna's mouth water. The whole apartment building must have smelled of anchovies for days afterward. A few pans were brought down to the Lancona household and a couple were kept for Gram and Marie and Jonna to eat. Even the next few days, even at room temperature, the taste was sensational. Those were great times of baking and bonding and learning the lost recipe that hailed from a specific area in Sicily.

Thanksgiving was super wonderful too. Grandma and Marie didn't consider this a religious holiday and were more comfortable joining in on the celebration.

Now Easter was another matter. They believed that it was not a Christian holiday. Once again, these beliefs set aside… for the sake of peace in the family. Bea was once again in her glory preparing colored eggs and chocolate bunnies for the Easter baskets they distributed. Jonna took part in some of the egg coloring. It was fun for her. Aunt Marge prepared a fresh ham, glazed and punctured with cloves. Her cooking was a hard act to follow.

When Halloween rolled around, it was another observance that involved witches, ghosts, goblins, black cats and other forms of sorcery and superstition very objectionable to Witnesses. However, Marie dressed Jonna up as a gypsy and Dennis as a pirate. They went around the building from door to door and floor to floor saying "anything for Halloween;" Marie didn't like the expression "trick or treat." One time, Marie dressed up in a white sheet with a pillow underneath and went around the neighborhood making ghoulish sounds.

New Year's Eve celebrations were also traditional affairs in the Italian style with homemade sausage prepared at midnight and a fish dinner early in the evening and finished with the usual array of pastries. Even though Dennis and Jonna were quite young, they were allowed to have a 7&7, Seagrams 7 whiskey and 7-up soda. Very light on the whiskey of course!

They watched the countdown broadcast from Times Square on the TV as the ball descended bringing the New Year. In Times Square hoots and hollars erupted as strangers hugged while being swayed by the burgeoning crowd in and around the bars and taverns.

The Lanconas opened up the windows and shouted Happy New Year into the quiet courtyard of mostly sleeping neighbors. Somewhere over the parkway on Villa Avenue, fireworks erupted with a profusion of color and loud blasts. Very exciting indeed!

Sometimes Jonna felt guilty participating in the festivities. She wasn't really able to reconcile being a Witness; and going along with these holiday celebrations. It seemed very hypocritical and made her uneasy. In many ways it was a curse to be brought up as a Witness, she felt like she was living two lives and not committed to one or the other.

Summer Ends.... School Starts

It was very hot that day. August summer dog days slowed down the world as the metal electric fans lazily blew the hot air back and forth. Air conditioning was not available yet, not for most people anyway.

Afternoons were still, the simmering asphalt and tar streets would bubble up like small volcanos erupting with black sticky stuff. Weak strains of a Yankee game wafted through the still air. Even the leaves were curling with no rain or breeze in sight, just heat. Most of the neighborhood kids were indoors or up at the Oval playground. The park offered a summer program for young children. The fees were relatively inexpensive. There was a shallow sloped pool spurting water like a fountain to the delight of the kids splashing and running through the cool shower.

On very rare occasions, the fire department would open the fire plug on Rochambeau Avenue. Plumes of cold water doused the street as the oily petroleum residue made blue and purple swirls on the hot pavement.

That week for before the start of the fall school year, everything was slowing down. Families who were away for the summer and kids who attended camp, slowly returned and life began anew.

PS 80 was diagonally across the street from Jonna's apartment building. Classes would begin the first Monday after Labor Day. It seemed like the days cooled down dramatically at that time of year. It smelled and felt like Autumn, only to have heat return in October which was called Indian summer.

Jonna loved the idea of going back to school. It was time for new clothes, school supplies and a new daily routine. Marie took Jonna shopping for the basics and some special school outfits. There wasn't an officially written dress code, but everyone seemed show up with similar outfits. Girls wore skirts or dresses and boys wore slacks and cotton or polo shirts. The school required gym bloomers for the girls, a one-piece light grey or tan costume, cinched at the waist and upper thigh. On auditorium day, the girls wore a middie blouse made of white cotton with a blue tie. These outfits were laundered weekly in preparation for the following week; everything had to be starched and ironed since there was no polyester back in the early-mid 50's. Cubes of starch were purchased at the local hardware store, dissolved in a basin with warm water. The clothes were dipped and swirled around and finally wrung damp and wrapped in a bath towel, ready to be ironed.

Then came the school supplies! Jonna loved the smell and feel of newly sharpened #2 wood pencils, the pencil box supplied with a sweet-smelling pink eraser, a small pencil sharpener, a few rubber bands and a small wooden ruler. She treasured the new 24-pack of waxy Crayola crayons nestled in their colorful paper sleeves awaiting some serious coloring and drawing on construction paper. How nice it was to have a new set of notebooks, one for each subject.

Other new items were white cotton socks, undies and finally a training bra. Jonna had no idea what a training bra was supposed to do. Was the almost flat bra supposed to train the slightly protruding breasts for better days to come? Puzzling.

The first day of school was a bit confusing. Kids were wandering through the halls, jousting and playful as they looked for their new teacher and assignments. Hallway monitors helped the students find their assigned classrooms. New and used books were distributed and a schedule outlined for the coming semester. They were taught arithmetic, geography, history, spelling and grammar, even a penmanship class. Social studies didn't come into use until the 7th grade when departmental changing of classes commenced. Shop and home economics were also offered along with couple of electives e,g. music, art.

The school was surrounded by three high concrete walls topped with a chain link fence. A sidewalk bordered the school yard as with most city schools. All the students walked to school, as most lived in a radius of about 6 blocks from the building. The high schools were much farther away. There was an adequate public transportation system in place and students were offered a discounted pass. Urban schools did not provide transportation as might be expected in the suburbs and rural school districts. Kids grew up fast; they became adept at navigating the city with public transportation.

Jonna was instructed to keep to herself, mind her own business, and not to socialize with other students. Child abduction was not at all that common: however, Marie made sure Jonna was fully aware and to keep alert for possible predators.

There may have been sports opportunities, but, here again, Marie believed that school was for learning the 3 r's, readin, writin, and arithmatic. Jonna was not on track for a career or higher education because it did not fit the picture and direction her life was to take. Marie regularly supplemented Jonna's education with home instruction on a variety of subjects. After school, after chores, after play and homework, Marie had her own lessons for Jonna to complete, like Bible study, word usage and sentence structure, word roots, how to balance a checkbook and a number of practical applications of everyday common sense. Although it may have seemed rudimentary, Jonna was prepared enough to enter the work force at an early age and contribute to the family income as was expected, following the path of the previous generation.

The School

Kindergarten was not mandatory at the time Jonna was attending school. In any event, Marie didn't want Jonna in the public school arena until absolutely necessary, so she started school in the first grade in September at five years old; she would be six in November. PS 80 was just a short walk across the street from her apartment on Rochambeau Avenue. There were no crossing guards and children were instructed to "look both ways" before proceeding through the crosswalk.

PS 80 and subsequently JHS 89 was rated among the top ten schools in the city at the time. Quite a few students went on to the Bronx High School of Science and other technical schools. Penny Marshal and Kevin Cline both attended PS80 and became famous in the entertainment field. They were a grade or two ahead of Jonna.

The classrooms were classic 1940's layout: they had wooden floors with somewhat battered wooden desks held in place with iron scrollwork that anchored them to the floor. There were 3 rows of desks, about seven deep, they had inkwells, and a lift top to store papers and books beneath, the seats folded back after school. Most of the classroom layouts were similar. Behind the teacher's desk was a blackboard, made out of slate. Above the blackboard was a pull-down laminated map of the world, somewhat frayed at its edges from use, the American flag hung off to one side. A typical morning routine included taking attendance and the reciting of the pledge of allegiance.

Jonna's favorite classes were geography, art, penmanship (yes there was a whole class devoted to penmanship), composition and writing. In Home Economics class she learned how to make cakes and buns and cookies. Another home ec class was devoted to sewing; Jonna made an apron of white muslin, piped with red finishing bias tape all around. It had a pocket too. All projects were done by hand sewing, using needle and thread.

Jonna had a bit of experience with sewing, practicing on Grandma Carmela's Singer treddle sewing machine brought from Staten Island. It was a simple but effective machine, the stitches were neat and regular, only straight stitching, nothing fancy. Patterns printed on tissue paper were purchased and ironed to remove the wrinkles. She learned to follow a simple pattern and completed several skirts with darts, zippers and waistbands.

In shop class, she made a battery operated device that lit up a light bulb when the wires were attached. Woodworking was fun too. She made book ends, stained and finished with lacquer for the shiny look. In art class, working with clay, ash trays with colorful glaze were brought home as a prize, very useful since lots of people smoked! Some projects in art class included gathering dried fall leaves and pressing them on construction paper between wax paper, the name of the tree leaf written at the bottom.

Another favorite subject was composition and poetry. With Marie's help, Jonna put together well-composed book reports and stories. In the early grades she wrote a poem and received an A for her effort:

> *"When summer starts to fade away, Autumn*
> *breezes blow our way... The ground cools off to set*
> *the course for cooler days and winter frost. The*

seasons change four times a year and each one
brings some kind of cheer... Autumn seems the
best of all, it ushers in a brand new fall."

In penmanship class, Jonna mastered writing with an ink fountain pen, held almost horizontally between index and middle fingers, with the other three resting on the page. She produced a flowing script, resembling hand writing of an earlier age.

During the Jewish holidays, the school emptied out since more than 85% of the kids were from Jewish families. Many teachers also observed those holidays. There were only a handful of kids in attendance. It was rather fun for them, since the regular routine was interrupted and assignments were few. They were told to clean the blackboards with felt erasers dipped in water to get off all the chalk. There was a lot of mischief making when the assignment turned into a game of toss the erasers and running up and down the aisles and hallways of the school; there was little supervision. One of the boys was named Dominic DeCaprio; he came from across the parkway on Villa Avenue. He was a cute, skinny Italian kid and Jonna had a crush on him. They chased each other around the classroom as pre-pubescent kids often did.

Jonna loved school. She was eager to learn and took pride in her grades and accomplishments. That love would change when she graduated from Junior High 80 and went to Walton High School. But that is another story told later on in this journal.

Linda

Linda Schildkraut lived on the sixth floor of the building in a 3-bedroom corner apartment. She was the only friend Jonna was allowed to have that met with Marie's approval. Perhaps the family met some approved criteria: they were a family of 4, husband, wife and 2 girls. They lived a conservative lifestyle and were apparently of moderate means. Mr. Schildkraut was a work-at-home architect and the missus was a first-class homemaker. The large apartment was always spotless; the plush dark green carpet showed vacuum cleaner lines and the beautiful furniture gleamed with sparkling crystal in the breakfront cabinet.

Jonna went up to Linda's a couple of times a week after school. Her Mom offered us a small glass of milk and an Oreo cookie for snack. Only one Oreo? Afterward, the girls made their way to the back bedrooms; one of which Linda shared with her sister Claire. Claire was retarded in some way and didn't speak; she only observed the girls at play. Their bedroom had 2 canopy beds covered with white eyelet ruffled canopies. Really pretty white girlie furniture filled the room. Maybe Jonna was envious when comparing these surroundings to her own. She did not have a bedroom, but slept in the living room on foam mattresses doubling as couches in the daytime.

Jonna brought her hairless baby doll that would be dressed and

59

undressed several times during play. The doll had eyes that opened and closed and cried something like maaama when put down. Linda had a doll carriage and crib with a pretty floral coverlet, a pillow and other baby stuff. They play-acted being mommies and cared for the dolls like they were real babies.

Sometimes, they dressed up in costumes and acted out being a dancer or movie star. Needless to say, their imaginations ran wild creating various scenarios for these characters.

Sometimes they played board games like Monopoly and Chutes and Ladders. Other times they played with paper dolls that had paper clothing cut outs. These paper dolls were purchased in a soft-cover booklet with complimentary clothing. Marie also taught Jonna how to make the cardboard dolls and paper clothing that was colored with crayons.

The other bedroom was a studio where Mr. Schildkraut plied his profession as architect/draftsman. It was a bright room with windows on two sides dressed with 2" metal venetian blinds, the kind with cloth tape separating the slats, functional but very hard to keep clean. Linda's family were conservative Jews, as were most of the people in the quiet neighborhood.

3191 Rochambeau Avenue was a pre-war building with six stories. Many of these buildings had professional suites on the ground floor. Doctor Sonnenberg had his practice in one of these ground-floor apartments on the North side of the building. The Lanconas got first class treatment when the doctor made house calls and cured almost anything with a shot of penicillin, the recommendation of taking 2 aspirins, and getting good night's sleep and to give him a call in the morning.

Dr. Steinberg's dentist office was just off the entrance, also on the north side of the building. Marie took Jonna twice a year for cleanings and whatever fillings were needed. Marie had developed a nervous disorder by this time and needed a shot of whiskey to calm herself. Dr. Steinberg provided the booze before he looked at her teeth.

Day to day

The matriarchal dominated environment that Jonna grew up in had some plusses and minuses. She was strongly influenced by Grandma Carmela because she spent quite a bit of time with her Gram. Marie left for work around 8:30 a.m. and didn't return until after 5:30 p.m.

Even at an early age Jonna prepared her breakfast, which often consisted of a tablespoon of cod liver oil. In addition, two egg yolks were added to a glass of chocolate milk and shaken together. Jonna was proficient at separating the egg whites from that white embryo-like stuff that was attached. In her older years, the yolks were stirred into a glass of sweet white wine. She often had a cup of coffee laced with sugar and milk.

The cod liver oil was stored in a small cabinet under the kitchen window; it was sort of a cold storage area. The thick white concoction came in a green glass bottle shaped like a fish. Another necessary supply stored there was a jar of some black thick gooey salve that looked like tar and was supposed to cure all sorts of skin ailments or outbreaks. Grandma called it medicina de troia and it came from the old country. The cabinet also housed a bottle of Rock n Rye, a bottle of dry red wine and a bottle of anisette licquor.

The only male authority figures in Jonna's life were her two uncles, Uncle Jerry and Uncle Sam. When Uncle Sam (Salvatore) visited a couple of times a month, Jonna would run and meet him and jump into his arms; he was her favorite; Grandma called him Toto, a common Sicilian moniker for Salvatore. Uncle Jerry and Aunt Marge lived around the corner on Mosholu Parkway. He worked a lot and Jonna didn't see him as often.

Before Marie left for work, she left a chore list that Jonna was to complete after school. It looked something like: Take out garbage. Go to little head (a grocer) and get ½ lb Swiss Cheese, ½ lb boiled ham thinly sliced and a ½ pound of Genoa salami. Go to Lessell's Drug store and get a bottle of alcohol and a bolt of cotton that was rolled and layered in blue paper, and a box of Henna pack hair coloring. This Henna was dry and then mixed with water to form a reddish-brown paste to color hair without chemicals; the use of Henna dates back to the Egyptian Empire several thousand years ago. One of Jonna's jobs was to prepare the henna pack and apply it to Marie's hair roots and hair once every 3-4 weeks. Marie's hair was a glimmering thick and wavy chestnut color with red highlights. The henna smelled earthy and herby like a strong tea.

Next, go to the fruit and vegetable stand and get some broccoli rabe, some ripe tomatoes, some green beans, an onion and a couple of potatoes, and as a treat some Bing cherries for herself. The butcher shop was next on the list; it smelled of sawdust which was scattered on the wooden floors. The meat cases had neat rows of steaks, sausages, chicken parts, pork chops and a nice assortment of meats. Jonna ordered veal cutlets specially trimmed and cut by Leonard the butcher. He knew Grandma's choice of veal cut on a special grain and pounded thin. These cutlets were dipped in egg, breaded and fried in butter. They came out so tender you could cut them with a fork. Deelishious!

Next stop was the Chinese laundry a few doors down from the hobby shop on Bainbridge Avenue. The list just said "Chinks" with the pink laundry slip attached. Jonna knew that meant pick-up and drop off the sheets. This service was a small luxury that was still affordable. The term Chinks was politically and even socially incorrect, but widely used during that time.

On the way home, pick up a pack of Luckies, the shortened form for Lucky Strike cigarettes at the candy store. The candy store owner knew Jonna and also knew the cigarettes were for her mother. No problem. They cost 25 cents.

On another day her chores included doing the laundry. The washers and dryer were in the basement of the building. Jonna disliked this chore most of all because the basement was disgusting. Galvanized garbage cans lined the hallway just outside of the elevator; they were stinking with rotting garbage waiting to be incinerated. The superintendent of the building was a portly, sweaty, pale-skinned lady whose daily costume included a stained dirty apron.

Twenty-five minutes later she went back down to the basement, collected the clothes and took the elevator to the 6th floor. The hallway floors were made of six sided small white tiles butted together with black cement. She took the worn marble stairway that led up to the roof door, which was coated with metal sheeting sometimes called a fire door. A steel arm secured the door that had a corresponding fitted latch.

The hot summer air hit Jonna like a furnace blast of heat in her face. Rooftops in the old buildings were coated with asphalt and tar between the roof panels. They gave off a choking creosote smell that took some getting used to. At about 15 to 20 foot intervals stood wind turbines, metal tubular stacks about 30 inches in diameter, that had curving vertical fans on top thereby releasing the building's heat into the air. There were vent poles all around where tenants strung clotheslines for hanging wet clothing. Jonna brought a bag of clothes pins and secured the damp clothing on the line. They dried quickly! About an hour later Jonna returned and loaded the dried clothing in the basket; the clothes resembled and felt like cardboard slabs but they also smelled of sun and fresh air.

She was now free to join the neighborhood kids for play on the street. They jumped rope, played with marbles that were carried in a cigar box that had square holes cut out allowing a good marble shooter to hit the holes dead on. The boys played stick ball, which was usually a broom handle, and when connected with the pinkie Spalding high bounce ball, sailed way down Rochambeau Avenue and were found days later nestled between car tires and the curb.

Hide and seek was also popular. One of the kids was blindfolded and spun around a couple of times and counted to ten... when he would shout "here I come ready or not" after removing the kerchief scarf. The idea was to tag the found kid before they returned to home base.

In the early evening, fireflies drifted on the warm evening air. The kids collected them in glass jars with holes poked in the top cap. The flies intermittently lit up and the jar glowed. Grasshoppers were caught too and also placed in one of those jars that had some dirt and grass in the bottom.

When there was no chore list, Jonna and Minnie Mouse, her toy fox terrier, went to the Oval Park; the park was only a block away from the apartment. She passed an old stone house on the left side of the street that looked abandoned and not cared for. In more recent years that building has been restored and the Valerian House is now the residence of the Bronx Historical Society.

While at the park, Jonna taught Minnie all kinds of tricks and obedience maneuvers with hand signals. Minnie sat up, Jonna threw a ball, and Minnie waited for the signal to retrieve.

In retrospect, Jonna's early years were spent without care or worry. The atmosphere was not hurried, and not threatening. During the 1950's it was a great time to just be a kid.

Friday nights

Friday nights were very special for Jonna. Marie regularly visited her sister-in-law, Aunt Marge, almost every Friday evening. Uncle Jerry was almost always working at night driving a taxi cab.

They lived on Mosholu Parkway just around the corner from Jonna's building. For several years they lived in a one bedroom, one bath, ground floor apartment; it had a living room/dining area all in one, with a galley kitchen. The big question was how did a family of five manage in the cramped space? The answer is with much difficulty and discontent.

Their 3 children, Bea, Gerald and Dennis occupied the only bedroom, with two bunk beds for the boys and a twin bed for Bea. Aunt Marge and Uncle Jerry used a pull out couch as their bed in the living/kitchen area.

Jonna, being an only child, had substituted Cousin Dennis for a brother. He was just 2 years younger. Besides meeting at the park for play after school, the Friday night play times were the best! They had imaginations that turned the small bedroom into a circus tent, a war zone, a cowboys and indians wild-west town. They would leap from the top bunk bed onto the twin bed pretending it was a trampoline. That bed took a lot of punishment!

The small step-stool was used as a pretend bar where the good cowboys met, had whiskey, and talked about their exploits. Outfitted with cowboy chaps and two six-shooters on a belt for fast draws, a cheap felt hat completed the outfit.

Another favorite scenario was a WWII reenactment. The main characters, Joe and Mike were played by the two wildly imaginative kids. The bed blankets were tented and held up by a broomstick where plans were made about attack on the Krauts. They were inspired by the plethora of benign war movies that hit the movie screen. The year was around 1953-1954. Jonna was 10-11 and Dennis was 8-9.

They reenacted shoot-out scenes from the westerns and invented a game called "fall the best." Dennis would draw his cap gun, ie, a six-shooter and Jonna would fall down in writhing agony. Then Jonna would shoot Dennis and he gave his interpretation of the wounded cowboy in his death throes. Aunt Marge and Marie would judge the falls and reward the winner with a treat. They essentially took turns as to who was the winner!

The adults were drinking coffee and smoking cigarettes in the kitchen area, gossiping and discussing life's turn of events, mostly complaining. Dennis and Jonna were so occupied with their play they didn't give a hoot about the grown-up conversation. Bea was 8 years older than Jonna and already out working. She joined the group after work and acted as another judge. Jonna remembers that cousin Bea was trying out for the NYPD, had taken and passed all the courses and was due to become a police officer when tragedy struck. She was completing the last course of the physical test, jumping a hurdle that was just about 25 feet from the finish line. When she landed, her foot twisted, and somehow she shattered her right knee and shin bone. Marie and Jonna visited her in Fordham Hospital during her week in recovery. Needless to say, she was disqualified from the job on the police force; she was heartbroken.

The following year the Lanconas moved to a larger 2-bedroom

apartment on the 5th floor of the same building. The building had two entrances, one on the north side and the other on the south. The new apartment had an entrance way to receive guests, to the right a small kitchen with an alcove dining area, and beyond a large living room… still only one bath. The difference between Jonna's building and Dennis' building were like day and night. The German super in Aunt Marge's building, kept the place immaculate, even the basement was freshly painted and maintained to spit and polish clean.

The Friday night get-togethers continued. By this time, a tv show called "Sea Hunt" starring Lloyd Bridges was showing on Friday evenings around 7:00 pm. Watching that show was the highlight of their week for Dennis and Jonna; both kids were fascinated by underwater adventures. The scenes and sets were really pretty lame in comparison to the later years of filming. But Jonna and Dennis were totally drawn in as Lloyd Bridges wrestled with a big water snake around some swaying seaweed!

One evening, after Sea Hunt, the two urchins went into the bathroom and closed the door. Jonna doesn't remember who came up with the bright idea of making spit-balls out of toilet tissue and hurling them out the narrow bathroom window hitting the back of the other building with a splat. They were having a ball trying to hit different parts of the wall, when suddenly the cocky doody hit the fan, so to speak. Someone in the other building squealed on them and reported the disturbance. Ben Wagner, the super, knocked on Aunt Marge's door and turned us in to the embarrassed parents.

This did not go over well at all. What they thought of as a fun game, turned out to be very painful for Dennis and mildly painful for Jonna. Dennis took a pretty good beating, but Jonna was given a good talking to and denied some future fun play with her cousin.

Evenings

The Lancona/Banderet family believed in being productive every day, so the evenings were filled with some creative project or other. Marie was determined to fill Jonna's spare time developing her imagination and creative instincts. After school, after chores, after outdoor play, after homework, after dinner, the projects would begin in earnest. The three generations, Grandma, mother, daughter hung out together in the small kitchen. One challenge was drawing faces with unusual proportions and putting a name to the face, then rating the drawing for 1st, second and third place.

Jonna had two 300-piece puzzles. She favored the western scene with a stagecoach and driver with mountains and desert foliage. That puzzle was done over and over until she could assemble it in a half hour! Simple games like wooden pick-up sticks or Jacks or card games were other regular evening activities. Schuppa and Briscola were Italian card games Jonna learned and mastered early. Grandma taught Jonna the strategy to play to win. By the way, an Italian deck of cards does not have the 8, 9 or 10 in the deck. They are substituted with Queen, Jack and King. Italian solitaire was also different; four rows represented the four suits; ten cards across were laid out. Grandma used to call the club suit "flowers." One card was turned over and replaced another card in the correct number order and suit. The idea was to get a row of each suit filled to the end where the king would be the last play. No strategy really. Amazingly, these games filled many hours with simple recreation.

Grandma would sing and teach Jonna Sicilian rhymes and stories. One was about a lost chicken left abandoned, poor chicken! Grandma recounted many songs from her teenage years when she and her sisters would change the lyrics and made up silly rhymes. Like the popular song… "In the shade of the old apple tree." They would say, she's got a shape like an old apple tree, with powder and paint all scattered around, and the dirt from her ears weighs a pound. You can see her false teeth hanging out and the rats of her hair coming through, yet she walks down the street and she thinks she looks neat; she's got a shape like an old apple tree, circa 1904.

Other times, they got the treddle Singer sewing machine fired up (no electric) and make simple clothing for everyday wear. The antique machine sat in a wooden desk-like enclosure where the sewing machine could be dropped down and stowed away. A wooden extension was swung over the top where a crocheted scarf was placed and some decorative bowls or glassware were displayed. Grandma had brought the old Singer from Staten Island to the apartment in the Bronx. Jonna really enjoyed turning a piece of cloth into something wearable. Marie made sure these small accomplishments were rewarded with praise and a hearty "well done."

Jonna always believed she was special. She was told repeatedly that she was beautiful both inside and out; the inside part being very important. After all, man sees the outside, but God looks into the heart.

Jonna felt secure during these years. Although there were strict guidelines and boundaries, she operated within her portion of life quite easily and contentedly.

She didn't have a care in the world.

Dominic

The swaying #4 bus ride to the Valentine Avenue stop at the corner of Fordham Road became routine for Marie. She worked in the Wagner Building on the Grand Concourse. Her boss, George Fretel, was easy enough to get along with and was hardly ever around; he left most of the operation to Marie. Jonna sometimes went to the office and learned telephone and general office procedure; Marie was a good teacher.

The Wagner Building was elegant for its day. The front entrance and lobby were decorated in Art Deco style, lots of marble with granite floors and walls. Two elevators served the five-story building. Krum's, the popular chocolatier and candy manufacturer, was located on the ground floor of the building and was the go-to lunch counter for Marie. They showcased fudge, candies, tarts and other sweets like the multi-colored and layered marzipan squares and the same sweet almond paste shaped like tiny fruit. Grilled cheese sandwiches were Jonna's favorite.

On the far corner of the building's ground floor was a newspaper cum candy store that offered all the usual fare. Cigarettes, magazines, greeting cards, dot candy on a white paper roll and such. It was just outside of the Fordham Road/Grand Concourse entry to the subway.

The whole area was a mecca for shopping. Across the Concourse stood Alexander's department store where almost everything could be purchased at moderate prices for decent merchandise. In later years Jonna had a part-time job at Alexander's in the linen department.

On one of her lunch breaks at Krum's, a casual observer noticed that Marie was engrossed in reading her Bible. Dominic R approached Marie and made introductions. He also worked in the Wagner Building and had an office just down the hall from Marie's; he had an insurance agency and accounting firm. That first meeting grew to more frequent meetings and they developed a sort of friendship that lasted many years. Dom was cordial and respectful when he visited the apartment and Grandma liked him. He brought Italian goodies for the family while Gram made Bustello brand expresso coffee in the pewter toned coffee pot. He always called Grandma signora Lancona. Once a year he did Marie's taxes pro bono and generously helped financially when she needed some extra help.

Jonna had no idea about the depth of their relationship. Marie was attractive and interesting but unavailable for a friendship of a more serious nature. Once a week or so, Dom would drive by the apartment and toot the horn outside to alert Jonna and Marie of his presence. Marie made some excuse to leave the house in the early evening, with Jonna in tow, and meet him. There was a diner on Broadway on the Bronx/Yonkers border where they spent hours talking, smoking and drinking coffee. Jonna was in her own world and hardly paid attention to the adult conversation.

Sometimes, Jonna and Marie met Dominic at the gazebo in the Botanical Gardens for lunch. He brought Swiss cheese, Italian salami and lettuce and tomato sandwiches on a crisp Italian bread, Jonna's favorite. Other times, they had lunch at the Snuff Mill, a newly constructed building in the Federal style. The upper floors probably contained management offices for the park. In the warmer months, colorful umbrellas dotted the terraced walkway that stretched down to a short stone wall bordering the Bronx River.

Their friendship lasted for several more years and Jonna has fond memories of the times spent with Dominic. He was a good friend.

The Botanical Gardens

Jonna never realized what a wonderful opportunity it was to live so close to the often visited Botanical Gardens of world fame. According to the Wikipedia post… The New York Botanical Gardens is a botanical garden at Bronx Park in the Bronx, New York City. Established in 1891, it is located on a 250-acre site that contains a landscape with over one million living plants; the Enid A. Haupt Conservatory, a greenhouse containing several habitats; and the LuEsther T. Merz Library, which contains one of the world's largest collections of botany-related texts.

NYBG is also a major educational institution, teaching visitors about plant science, ecology, and healthful eating through NYBG's interactive programming.

NYBG was established in 1891. The Lorillard family owned most of the land at that location. The city had been given the authorization to acquire the land as part of the 1884 New Parks Act, which was intended to preserve lands that would soon become part of New York City. Some 640 acres of land surrounding the Lorillard estate was acquired by the City of New York as part of Bronx Park in 1888-1889. The early fund raisers, the botanist Nathaniel Lord Britton and his wife Elizabeth Gertrude Britton, were inspired to emulate the Royal Botanical Gardens in London. The architecture emulated the Victorian Era style of the 1800's.

Jonna didn't know much about the history of the gardens at the time. All she knew was that it was a relatively short walk down Mosholu Parkway to the Southern Boulevard entrance of the park. There was no admission fee for pedestrians or autos entering the park during the week in the mid 1950's. Marie avoided weekend visits because there were more people circulating and she was not a fan of large gatherings.

Upon entering the gardens and to the left stood the library/museum that housed thousands of books, folios, botanical prints and other related publications. The first thing in sight was a 7-8-foot-wide slice of a Sequoia tree; the growth rings showed how old the tree was, over 300 years old, if Jonna remembers correctly. The separation between the rings indicated years of plentiful rainfall and dryer seasons. The wider the ring, the more rainfall for that period of time.

There were displays of early Indian life in glass enclosed cases along with the primitive cooking methods, clay pots and tools used at that time, and arrowheads, potshards, feathered arrows, partial animal skins that were used for clothing. The old yellowed tomes and leather-bound reference books smelled of dust and age. Everything was bordered with dark, thick wood that gave the feeling of stability and age-old comfort. Outside, there was a driveway that circled around the entrance with old growth trees and plantings lining the road and walkway. At the main road level was a large water fountain surrounded by a short wall to sit on and enjoy the cool spray on hot summer days.

The outer road along the high fence that circled the park led to the Conservatory with the 18th century design glass atrium that housed a variety of climate-controlled rooms featuring the fauna of a humid or jungle like environment and a hot house where desert and dry prickly plants thrived. The courtyard area accommodated two large rectangular pools filled with water lilies and lotus plants languishing in the dark water.

It felt special or even spiritual to stroll the walkways in this serene and calm setting.

When Jonna was in the 6ᵗʰ grade, the school organized a class trip to the Gardens. They were instructed about some species and plant habitation in the northeastern area. The event attracted the attention of the local newspaper where photographers poised to take some interesting shots to be reprinted in the paper. While waiting in the class queue, Jonna was approached by a photographer. He asked permission for Jonna to pose among the spring tulips. The teacher agreed as did Jonna. Sure enough, the photo appeared in the next days' local newspaper. Now that was exciting! She kept a copy of that picture for many years and it may have survived to this day in the archived boxes of photos stored in her children's attics.

When Jonna graduated from Junior High School, Marie took Jonna to the gardens for photos among the flowers and shrubs. She had a short haircut at that time and wore a white blouse and a white home-made linen skirt. It was Marie's idea of minimalist!

Shortly after that time, when Jonna was 13-14 years old, Marie taught her how to drive. During the day, in the gardens, when there was no traffic to speak of, Jonna learned how to drive. She learned quickly and would pinch hit for Marie when she wasn't able to drive as told in a later chapter.

There are so many memories to relate about the time spent in The Botanical Gardens. Let's just say that it felt like Jonna's private estate as she roamed the lanes and byways throughout the park. It was a special place where her thoughts could once again wander and explore where her imagination was set free to create elaborate stories and scenarios. Even today, as of this writing, Jonna is thrilled to reminisce about those wonderful times.

Saved by the birds

The local pet store on Fordham Road sold all sorts of critters and paraphernalia for their housing and care. Marie thought that Grandma Carmela needed an easy to maintain pet to take care of. She purchased a pair of colorful parakeets, a suitable cage, cuttle bone, bird seed and branches for the birds to stand on. By this time Gram had slowed down even more and was feeling abdominal pain and other discomforts. The birds served as a good distraction.

The bird cage and stand stood in a nook between the refrigerator and the dumb waiter door. The kitchen was small, but had built-ins, a pantry cabinet and a hutch that reached the ceiling, with wood surround enclosing glass panels, a space between the bottom drawers and lower cabinets.

Dumb waiters were installed in many of the pre-war buildings. Groceries were loaded on a platform made of wood that could be hauled up and down to each apartment operated by a pully system. This amenity went out of use for groceries and was used to lower garbage down to the basement. It also fell out of use, but the door could still be opened into the maw. The roaches had a highway from the basement to all the apartments in that line. The door was eventually sealed as a safety precaution. The nook for the birds measured about 3x3 feet.

Jonna was in charge of cage maintenance; the paper on the bottom of the cage was either newspaper or brown grocery bags, cut to fit and was changed daily. The birds were tame and would jump on an index finger to take a stroll around the kitchen. They did nip now and again, but not enough to draw blood!

In time, Marie purchased a much larger cage that looked like a pagoda to accommodate the increased bird population. The 6 birds were chirpy and noisy, but finally calmed down in the evening when the colorful cloth cover signaled "quiet time." During the day Grandma hummed and sang to the birds… they responded with enthusiastic chirping in reply.

Jonna asked for goldfish and turtles. In addition to her little fox terrier, "Minnie," she had a menagerie of critters to care for.

As was her routine, one afternoon, Grandma walked over to the cage to attend to the birds, changing water and adding food. Suddenly a loud crash like a cannon shot rang out from the kitchen. Marie and Jonna rushed to see what happened… Oh my God! Half of the kitchen ceiling had crashed down covering most of the center of the kitchen; it looked like a bomb was exploded! Grandma's hair and shoulders were covered in plaster dust as she stood motionless and in a daze.

The walls and ceilings of these pre-war buildings were made with plaster and lathe construction. Heavy chunks of this plaster were strewn throughout the kitchen, along with smaller pieces, destroyed the kitchen table, chairs and linoleum along with Gram's extra glasses.

After the dust settled, literally, the shock wore off and Jonna rushed downstairs to the basement to report the accident to the superintendent. The super came up to inspect and proceeded to remove the big pieces of plaster. Some pictures were taken for the report. The super helped with the clean-up, but it took several days to address the fine plaster dust all over everything including the dishes and foodstuffs in the pantry. What a mess!

The whole event would have been a perfect opportunity to sue the landlord for neglect, damages and trauma to Grandma. Instead the landlord offered compensation to the tune of $350.00 to cover replacement of damaged goods, including a new linoleum floor and new kitchen table and chairs. That amount was sufficient, and the family was content and grateful that Grandma was not severely injured or killed in the downfall.

In most Italian families the kitchen is the hub of life. It's the place where family disputes were settled, food prepared, coffee served, clothes ironed, and social activity planned; the kitchen carried the warmth and soul of the household. Fortunately, it only took a few weeks for the kitchen to return to normal and life went on as before.

Jonna at 18 months old.

Jonna at the Bronx Zoo. Circa 1948.

Jonna 6 years old at Oval Park.

Marie and Jonna up on the roof in the Bronx.

Part III

1954

Jonna was eleven years old and she would remember that year as the dawning of a new era, so to speak, in her young life. The comfort and security of life in her neighborhood and immediate surrounding neighborhoods were soon to be expanded to include life outside her Garden of Eden. If I'm sounding Biblical at this juncture, it is to make a point.

The year was 1954 and Marie bought a Chevrolet, coupe, 2 door, fleet grade, 6-cylinder automobile: the car cost about 1,500 dollars and came equipped with nothing. Literally. There was no heater, no radio, no air conditioning, no power steering, no automatic transmission, no white wall tires, in other words, stripped down to bare bones. It was a column stick shift with 1st, 2nd and 3rd forward gears and reverse. The grey cloth seats were scratchy and itchy to the thighs when wearing shorts. In the summer months the interior became so hot so as to melt anything plastic placed on the dashboard. This version of the Chevy was probably the cheapest new car on the road. Jonna remembers that Marie put up a small amount of money as a down payment and carried a note for three years. But hey, it was reliable transportation. The cars at that time were very simple to repair, change the oil, and maintain. Gasoline was 24 cents a gallon; it was leaded gasoline and returned very good gas mileage. Environmental issues notwithstanding, this transportation opened up a whole new world of travel and possibilities for the family, expanding their horizons to explore the land beyond!

The New York State Thruway had not been completed and they mostly traveled on state roads and highways. Quite a few of the roads were made of abutted concrete slabs where lesser traveled routes showed weeds springing up between the cracks.

One of their many destinations was to visit Aunt Marge where she worked. The company was called Schweirs Coal and Oil, where she did secretarial work and bookkeeping. Marie picked up take out coffee, (it was called regular coffee) standard fare with sugar and milk, and buttered rolls for their visit.

Often times, on Sunday, Jonna and Marie would enter Woodlawn Cemetery and explore the grounds with wonder. There were large mausoleums with gates and fancy wood doors, front pillars, some topped with lion heads or replicas of other animals, ornate ironwork and stained glass windows. The grounds were immaculate with old growth trees and plantings, making it seem more like an exclusive neighborhood than a cemetery. They brought their lunch and wandered around checking out the famous names of celebrities buried there. This one banyan tree, with huge branches and foliage reaching down to the ground, sprouted from a trunk that measured, guessing, about 5-6 feet in width, formed an umbrella-like enclosure; it felt so nice and cool beneath. This may seem like an eerie place to spend a Sunday afternoon, but Marie and Jonna had no superstitions about the dead and felt comfortable amidst the tombstones and burial sites. It was fun reading the names and dates of the departed and something about their family members also entombed.

While in these quiet surroundings, Marie gave Jonna another driving lesson. When alternative side of the street parking was in effect, Jonna was assigned to the early morning chore of moving the car from one side of the street to the other. Jonna became a whiz at parallel parking and almost always executed a 3-point landing.

The following chapters tell the stories and adventures that lie ahead for the inquisitive wanderers as they traveled beyond their realm to seek out the vast and interesting nooks and crannies in the wilds of Westchester County, the Bronx, New Jersey and surrounding hamlets and villages.

Exploring in the Chevy

One early afternoon, Marie, Jonna and cousin Dennis went for a ride up the Sprain Brook Parkway. It wasn't yet developed as a parkway back in that day, but was a wild and overgrown thicket; they almost had to hack their way through the dense growth. The brook was very much alive and flowing through the tangled vines. Dennis and Jonna took off to go exploring. Their minds wandered as they navigated the narrow paths. Maybe the trodden paths were from deer or other small critters, but clearly not heavily traversed.

Jonna was ahead of Dennis on the path and decided to sit down on a nice large flat rock. She was about to sit when Dennis shouted in an urgent voice "don't sit down, don't sit down." Jonna was startled about this warning. When she looked down, she finally saw what the warning was all about. A copperhead snake was lazily coiled on the warm rock apparently sleeping! She quickly retraced her steps and left the basking serpent undisturbed. That was a close one!

Other times they headed up the Saw Mill River Parkway which also had quite a bit of undisturbed grounds and paths. They brought picnic lunches and hiked around enjoying the almost wilderness feeling. Along the parkway, old Italian ladies were seen picking up the tender undisturbed dandelion plants. Jonna had never eaten dandelion and was curious about the wild plant and how it would taste. She sampled a few leaves…. Ummm very bitter indeed!

On Sunday mornings, Marie and Jonna took route 22 north to Armonk. The cider mill made fresh donuts on Sunday mornings. There isn't anything more enjoyable than a sweet warm cinnamon sugar donut just out of the fryer and a steaming cup of coffee. The farm property also sold freshly harvested seasonal produce. The emporium area offered all the typical country style accessories, home-made apple butters and nut clusters, fruit and such. There was an adjoining apple orchard where you could "pick your own" and pay for your harvest by the bag. The air was crisp and fresh with the fall weather approaching as the leaves also started to change color. In later years, Jonna took her own children on an annual fall apple picking pilgrimage. There were pony rides and face painting and spin art to entertain the crowds of visitors, a delightful way to spend an afternoon.

The annual winter trip up to White Plains happened in late December. The registration and plates for the Chevy had to be renewed in person at the motor vehicle bureau. Marie didn't like going into the city for this process and chose to renew at the White Plains location. Every year new license plates were purchased, the actual plates had to be replaced, one for the front and back of the bumper. In current times we speak of getting new "tags" instead of replacing the whole new plate. Eliminating thousands of used plates from the landfills is probably a good thing. Anyway, there was nothing like driving up to White Plains on a crisp snowy morning and to stop at yet another donut shop while waiting for the queue to slow down before getting in line.

Another annual event was to visit Nick the mechanic for a lube and oil change. Nick had only one bay to service cars. A pot belly stove sat in the corner of the shop regularly supplied with new logs to take the chill off the air. Marie and Jonna drank coffee and chatted with Nick as he performed the regular service. Nick would stick a lube gun into the ball joints of the Chevy and squeeze until the old dirty lubricant oozed out while the new grease took its place, a satisfying procedure!

The 1954 Chevy gave Jonna and Marie wings, so to speak. Well maybe not wings, but wheels none the less and they made very good use of this freedom as a few of the subsequent chapters will reveal.

Staten Island

Every six months or so, Grandma Carmela, Marie and Jonna headed down the West Side Highway in Manhattan to Bowling Green and the Staten Island Ferry. They were on their way to visit Aunt Mary, (Grandma's younger sister) and her children, Josephine, Lena, Rosemary and Salvatore, and Aunt Rose, Gram's older sister who did not have any children and lived alone. All three sisters were widowed at a relatively young age.

The Staten Island ferry was founded in the year 1817, continually operating on a 24 hour schedule, 7 days a week. It departs Whitehall in Manhattan and arrives at St. George, Staten Island on a half hour schedule. The ride takes about 20 minutes crossing the Hudson River for a bit over five miles; at that time the passenger fare was 5 cents for single passengers and 50 cents round trip for autos.

The docking slips were very old fashioned with green painted and scrolled overheads and buttresses, and curlicued iron works surrounding the gates and entryways; the whole area smelled of diesel fuel and accumulated grease. The water around the ferry was slick, forming circles of floating oil and created blue, purple and green swirls of color that stirred in the wake of departure.

It wasn't a long wait as the cars lined up awaiting entry onto the ferry.

The boat accommodated three lanes for cars loading the middle lane first and then the outer lanes alternately. Once aboard, Jonna immediately got out of the car and raced out to the rear railing to watch the ferry release its moorings from the dock and head out into the main channel of the Hudson. This whole experience was very exciting for Jonna and her imagination ran wild; this ferry might have been navigating the waters of the Nile or the Amazon. She soaked up the pungent smells of salty water and seaweed as she scampered along the aisles of cars noticing the ropes, buoys, and other equipment for ferry boats. Next, she went up to the concession stand for coffee and a hot dog for Marie and herself. The upper level of the ferry was open to the wind and sun with some seating. Grandma always stayed in the car napping or reading.

After the ferry docked in St. George on Staten Island, they wound their way around Richmond Terrace to Van Pelt Avenue, the old homestead of the Lanconas; the house was a modest two story colonial, painted a soft yellow. One time they stopped by the house and knocked on the door, introducing themselves as having one time lived in the house and complimented the new owners on how well kept and tidy it still looked.

Aunt Rose lived down the street in an apartment over a downstairs office and another storefront. Her husband was sort of a real estate tycoon. He was nicknamed "Don Pepe Palazzo" and recalled as being somewhat of a dandy. After his death Aunt Rose owned the whole building and lived rent free.

The upstairs apartment was small with low ceilings and furnished with antique furniture purchased many years before. Under lamps and ornamental vases, doilies of different sizes and colors protected the surface of the end tables. The armchairs were adorned with hand crocheted antimacassars, an invention dating from 19th century England; macassar was a hair oil for men to keep their hair down and in place. If the men would rest their greasy heads on the back of the couch, the oily substance would leave a permanent stain. Ergo antimacassar!

Jonna snooped around the downstairs former real estate office and played with the pens and paper and other office supplies, while the grownups talked and drank coffee and dipped biscotti in the brew. On other occasions, Marie and Jonna visited Aunt Rose during the blistering summer heat in the city and escaped to the countrified environs of Staten Island. They walked to the town pool on an almost deserted street to take a cool refreshing dip. A nice get-away.

The next stop was Aunt Mary's where a banquet was being prepared for their visit. Aunt Mary lived in a quaint modest home on a small lot surrounded by overgrown shrubs and trees. A small entryway with a set of stairs leading up to 3 small bedrooms to the left; to the right of the entrance was the "parlor" or living room and behind that was a formal dining room with buffets and china cabinets lining two walls. Jonna was impressed by this furniture and décor. Although it was not extravagantly appointed, it felt warm and cozy.

Now the kitchen was another thing! There sat a wood/coal stove like what was found in rural areas throughout the country. On the rear kitchen wall stood built-in cabinets with drawers containing everyday tableware, cloths and flatware. It was cheerful and inviting. Early in the morning Aunt Mary loaded the stove with coal and wood, feeding it all day.

The big pot of tomato sauce with meatballs, sausage, brasciole, pieces of beef and pork was on a low simmer for several hours with a little sugar and red wine added toward the end of cooking. Everything was fresh and homemade and it was wonderful. Jonna listened to stories about the "old days" and learned quite a bit about the history of the immigrants. Aunt Mary was blind in one eye, damaged by a fork poke in her youth; it looked milky and greyish blue.

While the grownups in the kitchen talked and drank coffee the kids did what kids do… play. The small back yard was great for play with a long roped swing fastened up in a tree. Wildflowers grew in a profusion of color that attracted butterflies and birds and bees! The stone water font was slimy with algae, but the birds didn't seem to mind at all.

Finally, everyone was called to dinner. Out came the "better" china as the family gathered around the table. The meal was served in a few courses starting with pasta, then the meat, then a green vegetable accompanied by fresh baked Italian crusty bread. They lingered over conversation, wine, nuts in the shell, cheeses, coffee, anisette liquor, pastries and desserts, a veritable feast that carried on into the night.

Aunt Mary and Grandma knew some sleight of hand card tricks and games. A mythical character called "Belickita Beloketa" would hide coins around the dining room and the kids would search for the hidden treasure. Italian card games were played into the night.

Although it was late in the evening, Marie decided to get back to the Bronx anyway. The Chevy was loaded with a supply of leftover dinner and dessert as the good byes and hugs delayed departure.

They retraced their way back to the ferry terminal. There were only a few cars in the queue, and were quickly loaded on to the ferry to make the crossing to the Manhattan side. The return trip, up the West Side Highway, over the Henry Hudson Bridge and to the Saw Mill River Parkway, exiting at Mosholu Parkway, was uneventful. They were tired and after unloading, bedtime was overdue. It would be another 6 months before they repeated this ritual.

Jonna didn't realize how precious those get togethers were until she was older. Much older. Although she carried some of these traditions with her own family, they had lost their potency because the previous generation of older immigrants had passed.

Those memories stayed with Jonna for many years to come, well into adulthood. Good family times provided a sense of security and a place of belonging.

Annual Vacation

The city was hot and humid and breezeless; the old metal fan moved the hot air from one area of the room to the other, coating everything with more soot and dust. It was time to escape and head for the hills!

Destination: Phoenicia in the Catskills. Marie scheduled her annual vacation to coincide with Uncle Jerry's and Aunt Marge's summer vacation time.

After the cars were loaded up with everything one might need during this get-away, they steered north along the east side of the Hudson, up route 9, over the Bear Mountain Bridge, connecting with 9W continuing up to Kingston. Parts of the road were carved out of the mountainside and Grandma closed her eyes and said a silent prayer for our safety navigating this treacherous stretch of road.

After crossing the bridge, the state road continued up the west side of the Hudson, passing West Point. Along the way, local farmers and merchants displayed their bounty in roadside stands, featuring home grown tomatoes, summer squash, seasonal fruit and vegetables. They offered homemade pies and pastry goodies, bread, jellies and jams. The Lancona/Banderet caravan stopped a few times to stretch and pick up some supplies. It's no wonder the trip took all day!

At Kingston, route 9W intersected with route 28 with a westward heading toward their destination, Phoenicia. There were more shops along the way, selling all sorts of hand-made items, souvenirs, and one whole store was dedicated to doll houses. These doll houses were no plastic Barbie doll fare but meticulously wood crafted and ornamented in the Victorian style of architecture and design. Some stood 4 feet tall with interior staircases leading up to bedrooms and attic space. They were furnished with scaled down representations of typical furniture and decor of the late 1800's. Jonna marveled at these buildings and wished to have one of her very own. That wasn't happening since these miniature houses were very expensive, besides, they would take up too much room in a small apartment.

The caravan continued into the town of Phoenicia. Aunt Marge stopped at McGrath's supermarket to pick up the week's supplies and foodstuffs. It was getting late into the afternoon when they turned into The Phoenicia Motor Court. There were a few attached cabins and separate cabins of 1 and 2 bedrooms, some with full kitchens and dining/living area. Grandma, Marie and Jonna had the smaller version, a one bedroom and small living area with a pull-out couch.

They no sooner arrived, when Cousin Dennis and Jonna scampered down to the brook. In retrospect, it's amazing how their parents allowed these two very young kids to wander off through the woods alone and unattended. Jonna was 11-12 years old and Dennis two years younger. Jonna and Dennis didn't have a lot of "stuff" in their lives, but it allowed them the opportunity to use their imaginations which took them far and away beyond their immediate environment. They became explorers, travelers, pirates and captains of ships, journeymen, soldiers and Indians, hobos and scamps.

The old rickety trestle bridge that crossed the Esopus Creek had a center pilon or support made out of natural stone and concrete, with a sort of staircase down to the platform and the creek. Sometimes the water moved lazily along and sometimes the swift current would take a swimmer downstream where you could gingerly cross over rocks on shore and get back to the bridge. Jonna told Dennis, "you jump in the water first and scare the fish!" then I'll come in. The freshwater streams, brooks and rivers had an abundance of trout and fishermen could be spotted hip deep in the current trying their skills to outsmart the crafty fish. The old question: why are fish so smart? The answer... because they travel in schools! Very funny.

The afternoon sun dipped behind the tall trees and almost immediately it got cool. Uncle Jerry was busy setting up the charcoal bar-b-que grill, a simple first night dinner followed.

Marge and Sevie owned the cabins and the adjoining restaurant. According to the elders, they served the best ham sandwiches in the world, and indeed they probably were! Mostly, Aunt Marge did the cooking and prepared wonderful meals in the German and Italian style. She made the best mashed potatoes and gravy and beef brisket and a Sicilian tomato sauce to knock your socks off!

Jonna does remember Aunt Marge and Marie sitting around the kitchen table in the cabin, smoking and drinking coffee. That was her break time, while the aroma of simmering dinners wafted through the open cabin windows. Jonna suspected the neighbors were drooling!

After dinner, after dessert and coffee and pastries, the stories began, card tricks and games were played. Uncle Jerry told a story in Sicilian about a wily wolf, a lupo, who outsmarted the hunter over and over. His double barrel shotgun surely had the wolf in sight, when he squeezed the trigger and missed altogether. The frustrated hunter uttered some expletives while the crafty wolf snickered behind a tree. Marie translated the story into English.

Some evenings the clan went out for dinner at Al's Seafood and Steaks bar and grill, a popular local hang-out and watering hole. Some of the old timers greeted the family, remembering them from the old days.

In town, Froelich's emporium sold fishing gear and German coocoo clocks that had a boy and girl come out on the hour and dance in a circle to a Bavarian tune. There were wooden cigar store Indians, leather tooled and beaded purses and belts, cowboy hats, hunting knives in tooled scabbards, and little Indian girl dolls with long black braids, beaded headdresses, and calf-hide dresses. Aunt Marge told Jonna to pick out something that she would like to have and one of these Indian maiden dolls became her treasured gift!

The annual pilgrimage to Phoenicia went on for several years and into Jonna's early teens.

As grownups, in later years, Jonna returned to the old camping grounds with Cousin Bea and her boyfriend Ken, Dennis, Aunt Marge, Gram and Marie. One trip, they decided to raft down the Esopus Creek in three blow-up rafts. Bea was all suited up with a life preserver vest; she didn't know how to swim. They set off in slow shallow water and drifted into the current which at first was calm and easily navigated. Soon the waters swiftly grabbed the blow up boats, increasing their speed, swirling around boulders, tossing the boats forward and backward and sideways. Bea was beginning to panic, and then the worst happened. Her boat skimmed a sharp rock and punctured a hold in the side. The air quickly leaked out and the flat raft overturned spilling Bea in the swift current. Jonna, Dennis and Ken made it to shore with their boats. Meanwhile Bea was careening down mid-stream, flailing in the deepening water.

Dennis reacted immediately and swam out grabbing Bea by the life vest and slowly maneuvered her to shore a ways downstream. Bea was unharmed physically, but looked like a ghost from the fright of the experience.

The Neubauers

Marie became acquainted with the Neubauers around the year 1956, through a brother, Milton Weiss, who was a rabbi before he converted to the Jehovah's Witness sect. Milton made "shepherding calls" to encourage Marie and Grandma since they were not regular attendees at the Kingdom Hall. On one of these visits, he suggested that Marie and Jonna meet Una and Arthur Neubauer; he would make the introductions.

Una was a "sister in the truth" and had been baptized several years before. She was unable to attend meetings at the Kingdom Hall. Arthur, on the other hand, had not made any such commitment but remained tolerant of his wife's decision. Una was home-bound for several years, suffering from a chronic breast tumor that rendered her virtually incapacitated. The tumor was being treated with a greenish salve covered with a cloth dressing. Her family hailed from Sweden.

Arthur had German ancestry, his occupation was head baker at Arnold bakery, located in Brooklyn. He commuted, via subway, every day into the city and into Brooklyn. As a typical New Yorker, Arthur didn't own a car and never had owned one and didn't even know how to drive. There was a men's club in the city that he sometimes frequented where he met Fred Astaire and a couple of other high profile entertainers of the day. He managed to hob nob with some of these folks because they shared a love of horse racing. Arthur said that horse racing was "the sport of Kings."

The Neubaurs lived in the Kingsbridge section of the Bronx, just off of Kingsbridge Road in a 6-story walk up corner apartment. It was a fairly large apartment with an entry foyer, bedroom to the left of the entrance, a small kitchen with dining area followed. The front living room was furnished with traditional furniture and carpeting. Some of Una's paintings were positioned over the couch. Many of these pre-war buildings had decorative wall moldings with sconces between the moldings. Arthur's bedroom and bathroom were situated at the end of a hallway.

After being introduced, Marie and Jonna visited the Neubaurs weekly. They tiptoed around the kitchen, holding their skirts so as not to touch the floor. Keeping a clean house was last on the Neubauer's mind, there were lots of roaches around. When they visited, besides making juice for the week, they cleaned up the whole kitchen.

The Neubauers had started a juicing program after purchasing an expensive extractor from Milton. Milton was some kind of health guru and touted the benefits of juicing green leafy vegetables, carrots, celery and a variety of other veggies. Apples were sometimes added for sweetness.

At that time, Marie was having abdominal cramps, probably menstrual, and her life was interrupted by this intermittent pain. The consensus of opinion was that she had an impacted colon and needed to take daily enemas. She read a book that illustrated an autopsy photo of a twisted and terribly impacted colon, which according to the author, led to every ailment imaginable and that a clean colon would "cure a headache or cancer."

Arthur purchased a juicer for Marie and Jonna and Gram. Marie arranged weekly trips to the Bronx produce market in the Hunts Point section. Daddy Neubauer, as Una called him, would purchase a trunkful of vegetables to be divvied up when they got home. Jonna was put in charge of vegetable cleaning and juicing on a daily basis. After the juice was stored in glass bottles and refrigerated, Jonna had to clean the juicer of accumulated pulp. She grew tired of this after a few months and began to slack off; Marie did not show any noticeable signs of improvement, neither did Gram. Jonna was a healthy kid and already full of energy and vitality; the quarts of juice ingested daily didn't make much of a difference in the quality of her life.

To help Marie with the pain, Milton put her feet in a tub of iced water and squeezed each toe to promote healing. Umm, this unorthodox treatment didn't work either; Marie's intermittent pain continued.

During the next few years, Daddy Neubauer asked Marie to act as chauffer for him when he wanted to go to the track. Roosevelt Raceway was located in Queens and was about a 20 minute drive from lower Manhattan. The nighttime races featured racing for trotters and pacers. The pacers were hobbled with leather straps so that the front and rear leg on the same side moved forward together. The jockeys sat in sulkies and lined up behind a movable gate that was released to start the race. Mostly the threesome hung out in the stands. Arthur gave Jonna money to place a bet on the selected steed before each race. He waited to see how the odds moved on the tote board and this helped him determine the bet. An odds-on favorite paid 3-2. A bettor who placed a $200 bet got a return of $300 if the horse won.

During the preceding week, Arthur studied the horse racing stats in the newspaper and followed the horses' track records as they raced on tracks across the country. He researched the pundits, but mostly did his own handicapping. He taught Jonna how to read a racing sheet and pointed out that some of the horses performed well on muddy tracks, appropriately called mudders; others liked a dry hard packed surface. When he felt that a horse was "ready," he called Marie and asked for a pick-up down in the city near Canal Street. Jonna was around 15 years old, posing as a grown-up on these adventures. It was fascinating to listen to Arthur talk about the old days of horse racing and how there were bookies at the tracks offering odds and taking bets; a bettor could shop around for the best offer. That form of betting was replaced by parimutuel electronic betting.

Jonna's favorite racetrack was Belmont Raceway (this form of racing is called the "flats") located in Elmont, NY. Belmont Racetrack is one of three major racing parks in New York: Aqueduct, located in Ozone Park Queens, Belmont Park and Saratoga, located upstate New York in Saratoga Springs. Belmont opened May 4, 1905 and maintained the elegance of old-time racing; it hosts the third leg of the Triple Crown called The Belmont Stakes. The Kentucky Derby, held at Churchill Downs in Kentucky is the first race. The Preakness held at Pimlico Racetrack in Baltimore, Maryland, is the second race. Although the 1930's and 40's saw a waning of attendance at the tracks, by the 1950's and 60's it was again in full bloom, attended by many fans.

Jonna loved Belmont Park because it was full of trees and green areas especially around the paddock. The grooms paraded the sleek and polished horses around the oval where racing fans got a close-up look at the horses preparing to race. In the middle of the paddock stood a statue of Secretariat, one of the most famous of all Triple Crown winners. Jonna thought these beautiful horses knew that they were special with their combed manes and swishing tails; they moved like the thoroughbreds that they were. Some had their legs wrapped, some were skittish and had on blinders.

One time Arthur made reservations at the Garden Terrace dining room on the fourth level of the stands overlooking the track and the finish line. Proper attire was requested and many of the guests were outfitted in their finery. How exciting! Jonna was exposed to the privileged enjoying the pomp and circumstance their privilege afforded.

The jockeys were mounted and slowly steered their horses onto the groomed track. A machine came by after each race and raked the dirt into smooth ridges eliminating the hoof divots. They looked confident and slicked out in the identifying silks of the horses' owners. All of the jockeys were very small in stature and weighed under a hundred pounds; a good number of them were from South or Central America. A couple of exceptions were Willie "Willie the Shoe" Shoemaker was born in Fabens, Texas, and Bill Hartack, born in Cambria County, Pennsylvania.

As the horse and jockey moved into the gate, the race caller would announce "it's post-time," indicating the start of the race. When the gates were lifted, the caller again announced "and they're off" and, for example, he would call, "and its White Lightening taking the lead with Harry's Heart in second coming up on the rail, with Charlie Brown in third and so on until the last horse say Black Beauty in last position. He proceeded to call the race as the horses jockeyed for position heading into the turns and the stretch to the finish line.

The jockeys tapped the horses with their whip, spurring them on to a burst of speed in the stretch. The fans rose up and cheered their horse saying "come on Charlie Brown" or "don't give up Black Beauty." The excitement among the bettors was palpable as the galloping horses, kicking up clumps of dark brown dirt, showed their stuff toward possible victory. Sometimes there was announced a photo finish where two horses were neck and neck into the stretch and reached the finish line almost simultaneously. An electronic photo was taken to determine the winner. The caller would finally announce the winner, let's say, "by a nose."

The jockeys dismounted with all their gear to be weighed and the horses were given a saliva test to determine if any drugs were used to enhance their performance.

In 1973 OTB (off track betting) opened and the tracks began to lose attendance. These betting parlors were operating at several locations throughout the city. Jonna didn't like the idea and felt that betting was only a part of the horse racing experience. She was a romantic in nature and appreciated the smells, sounds, sights and feel being a part of the process of living. A good deal was lost when watching a screen presentation; it was unable to convey the sensory input she treasured.

To say that Jonna was thrilled by these experiences at the track is an understatement. From her perspective, during the teenage years, the whole aspect of being in an adult world, behaving as an adult, and leaving the torturous growing up stuff to the other kids suited her just fine.

In many ways Arthur was a class act. He wasn't a smart dresser and oftentimes appeared unkempt and a bit wrinkled. As was the common style, back in the day, Art wore a fedora, a suit, or a suit jacket with slacks.

He was very generous with his winnings at the track and often gave Marie bonuses as compensation for her chauffeuring; Jonna thought that he enjoyed their company too.

Every couple of months, Arthur invited Marie and Jonna to a special outing in the city. One of those invitations was to dine at the Café Carlyle in the Carlyle hotel.

Note: The golden age of NY cabaret comes alive each night at Café Carlyle. With an authentic Manhattan backdrop and a soundtrack that is classic cabaret. The Hotel had hosted everyone from Lucille ball and John F. Kennedy to Bono and Naomi Campbell since its doors opened in 1930. Bobby Short, a cabaret singer that embodied NY style and sophistication, was a fixture at his piano for more than 35 years.

Arthur, in his typical fashion, ordered a 12 year old scotch and a steak dinner. Marie and Jonna followed suit and ordered similarly. They were catered to in high style while Bobby Short tinkled the ivories. Jonna was introduced to Benedictine and Brandy for after dinner libation served with a delicate flaky apple torte for dessert. Everything was luscious. Jonna was sort of rubbing elbows with the upper crust of Manhattan's elite, another experience stored away in her memory bank.

Sometimes, they met Arthur a little earlier, before the nighttime races, and patronize an authentic Chinese restaurant on Mott Street, just off of Canal. Once again, they were treated to the best that Chinatown had to offer. After dinner they perused the shops where Jonna spotted a beautiful shiny light green Chinese style dress. She ogled the dress for a few minutes, when Arthur offered to purchase the dress. The clingy dress showed off Jonna's slim size 8 figure in a mildly seductive way. It was just so special and kept in reserve for special occasions.

Another memorable occasion was when Arthur invited Marie and Jonna once again to dine out, this time at the Plaza hotel. The Plaza is located at Fifth Avenue and Central Park South and was built in 1907 at a cost of $12 million dollars – an unprecedented sum in those days. The 19-story skyscraper of its day was touted to be "the greatest hotel in the world" and it may have been so when it was built. Famous persons, presidents, kings and influential society elite relished the pomp, glory and opulence of the French-style chateau.

Alfred Hitchcock's thriller North by Northwest released in 1959, marks the first time the Plaza was prominently featured on the big screen. It takes place in the Oak Bar, where Cary Grant gets kidnapped, but then quickly escapes through the 59th Street entrance.

Many years later in 1992, the Plaza was once again featured in the Home Alone 2 movie. Macaulay Culkin (Kevin) stays at the Plaza un-chaperoned while he is lost in NY and hijinks ensue.

The 2013 film "The Great Gatsby" starring Leonardo Decaprio as Jay Gatsby had its climactic scene filmed at the Plaza

Jonna doesn't remember what dining room they dined in that evening, only that it had an orchestra and dance floor surrounded by candlelit tables. The food and drink was excellent with two waiters at their beck and call. The music started and finely dressed couples waltzed around the dance floor. Another jazzy tune was played and Marie coaxed Jonna to get up and dance with Arthur. Arthur reluctantly agreed because he didn't know how to dance. In spite of that, Jonna and Arthur made their way to the parquet dance floor. Poor Daddy Neubauer was like a fish out of water as he stood almost not moving while Jonna did her interpretive dance around him, making somewhat of a spectacle of herself.

The music ended and they returned to their table. A few minutes later, a tuxedoed maître d' approached the table and said "have you noticed that the music has stopped?" and that "it would not resume until they left the table and the dining room." Ouch and double ouch. Arthur was very embarrassed, Jonna was embarrassed and Marie must have gone pale; a very disappointing end to what could have been a wonderful evening. Arthur paid the bill, they gathered up their belongings and exited the ballroom with their heads held high.

On the way home, they discussed the incident and couldn't figure out why this happened and felt that the hotel management was out-of-line.

As the years passed and Jonna recalled the incident with friends, she jokingly boasted about how she was, in so many words, "thrown out of the Plaza."

1958

In the summer of 1958, a week-long International Convention of Jehovah's Witnesses was held at Yankee Stadium. This convention was the first and last of its kind. Brothers and sisters from all over the world attended the highly visible and well-documented event. News reports daily flooded the tabloids with stories and accounts of the progress, talks, study book releases and dramas presented throughout the week. Jonna remembers one of the dramas was about David and Bathsheba. Big lessons there!

The stands were full, way up into the nosebleed seating at the stadium. Many endured the hot, sunny days seated in the bleachers. Long queues of sweaty folks awaited their lunch at one of the many hot dog and hamburger and pizza stands throughout. The overflow crowd camped out in the hallways and corridors and under the eaves of the stadium with lawn chairs and blankets and bedding for children, coolers and thermoses filled with milk, sodas and coffee. At that time, there was no bottled water for sale, but there were many water fountains throughout the stadium.

All were welcome and no charge for entry imposed. Contribution boxes were located throughout the stadium and books, bibles, journals and magazines were available for sale. It was well organized and efficiently run considering the throngs of faithful followers and others who attended, including those studying or just curious. Reporters with flash cameras documented the proceedings, interviewing and recording experiences of the attendees who traveled from distant lands, some dressed in their native costume.

Months before the event, Marie contacted the Watchtower Bible and Tract Society located in Brooklyn and offered to host a guest from overseas. She requested a French-speaking woman. She was informed that a woman from French-speaking Heliopolis in Egypt was seeking a place to stay in the city not too far from the stadium. Her name was Marguerite Tewfik or Tewfiq; they were introduced by letter, and arrangements were made for her to stay at the apartment for about 10 days.

Marguerite was a short, round, happy-faced woman in her mid-thirties or so. Some of the Witnesses who came from religiously oppressed countries expressed joy and happiness to be in the US where there was religious freedom. Marguerite showered Marie and Jonna with beautifully hand crafted silver Egyptian jewelry, some with inlaid semi-precious stones, as an expression of thanks for their hospitality.

Grandma, Marie and Jonna and Marguerite drove down to 161st Street in the Bronx, and parked on the street near the stadium. Tents with vendors and food service were set up outside to handle the throngs of people. Marie and Grandma did not attend every session of the assembly; Marie disliked crowds and Grandma was not physically well enough to endure the heat and stress of the gathering. On those days, Marguerite took the subway and exited at the Yankee Stadium stop at 161st Street and the Grand Concourse, a short walk to the arena. The highlight of the 7-day event was on Sunday when new books and bibles were released. The roar of the crowd showed their approval and enthusiasm for the efforts of the ministerial body to prepare and present these publications.

The theme of most of the literature announced the Kingdom rule of Jehovah God through His Son Christ Jesus. They highlighted the Scriptures that spoke of the signs of the last days and the tribulation that would be experienced, leading up to the final battle of Armageddon where Christ would be victorious over Satan and the forces of evil he represented. The nemesis would be chained up for a 1000 years with no access to the faithful and righteous worshippers on earth. This period of time would see the earth restored and brought back to Eden-like conditions, where there would be peace and plenty, where the inhabitants thrived under a just and fair government without fear of oppression, thereby allowing them to grow in knowledge and wisdom to the communal benefit of all. Isaiah was often quoted: "They will beat their swords into plow shears and spears into pruning hooks." By the way, this quote from Isaiah is engraved on a stone wall outside the United Nations Building in Ralph Bunch Park. Also a bronze statue of a muscled man holding an iron mallet smashing the swords into pruning hooks is also displayed around the courtyard of the United Nations building.

As an expression of non-violence, the whimsical Swedish artist Carl Frederik Reutersward, created a sculpture of a pistol with a knotted barrel which would become an international symbol of peace. Originally, the brass sculpture was erected in Strawberry Fields in Central Park located across the street from the Dakota, the apartment building where John Lennon was shot to death. Years later a replica of this sculpture was placed in the courtyard of the UN, another silent tribute to peace on earth.

Meanwhile, back at the small apartment, it was a tight squeeze accommodating their guest from Egypt. Jonna and Marie gave up their sleeping quarters in the living room so that Marguerite would have her own space and some privacy. They made do sleeping in Grandma's double bed for 10 days. Grandma was on the right side, Marie on the left and poor Jonna in the middle. She was to be absolutely still so as not to disturb Marie and Grandma. Minnie, Jonna's toy fox terrier slept in her bed on the floor.

It was terribly uncomfortable and distressing for Jonna. Grandma Carmela was not particular about personal hygiene, and with the cramped space her body odor was nauseating to Jonna. It was from that experience that Jonna developed claustrophobia and would recoil at being in tight spaces. Although Jonna did not realize how the trauma of that event would influence her throughout the coming years, it manifested itself by her not wanting to be touched and seeking to be separate, allowing breathing space. Perhaps this event, stored in Jonna's memory, contributed the chronic pain disorder that plagued her many years later. The body remembers!

Jonna was almost always put in a position to sacrifice her own comfort to allow others to be comfortable and undisturbed by her presence. These attitudes, drummed into Jonna's head from very young, were, at the very least, over-the-top, so to speak, and it would take the greater part of a lifetime for Jonna to understand that she was entitled to likes and dislikes and that it was not wrong to have personal preferences come before those of others. She was in her 60's before the door opened and she was able to make her way in the world anew, experiencing the freedom to be as curious as she pleased. With this new-found liberation, the adventure of a lifetime began to unfold as her horizons expanded and her perspective widened.

Florida

Chasing Sinatra

The movie "A Hole in the Head" starring Frank Sinatra, Edward G. Robinson, Thelma Ritter and Eddie Hodges hit the movie theaters around the Bronx in 1959. An immediate hit, the story was about a down and out small hotel owner on Miami Beach (Tony Manetta) and his adorable son (Ally). It was a musical of sorts; the song High Hopes aired to the delight of movie going audiences. Marie and Jonna chased the movie all around the Bronx and Upper Manhattan. Most theaters offered double features at that time and A Hole in the Head was shown with "Some Like it Hot" starring Tony Curtis, Marilyn Monroe and Jack Lemon, one of the best movie comedies to ever hit the cinema screen. Marie and Jonna saw that duel presentation at least 12 times and knew every gesture and line in both. They cruised down the road singing and reciting lines from both movies that they had committed to memory.

During this same time frame, Frank Sinatra and the legendary "Rat Pack" had made their mark in the entertainment venue in Las Vegas, Nevada. This group was featured in the movie "Ocean's Eleven" with Dean Martin, Joey Bishop, Peter Lawford, Sammy Davis Junior and others, who comprised the exclusive group of entertainers. They saw this movie multiple times as well.

It was a hot day in August when Marie got the idea to take a road trip to Florida to look up the hotel where the movie "A Hole in the Head" was filmed. So in the summer of 1959, the motley crew consisting of Marie, Grandma, Jonna and Minnie were loaded into the Chevy, crossed the George Washington Bridge, picked up the New Jersey Turnpike and began the long hot ride down south. Interstate 95 was barely completed and only small sections were drivable. So, mostly they took secondary roads and state highways. It was slow going and they made it a 4 day trip, staying in cheap motels along the way. It was at a stop in South Carolina, at yet another flea bag motel, that Jonna noticed a really bad smell in the room. It turned out to be coming from the water that smelled like rotten eggs. The area had lots of sulfur in the water causing the gagging smell.

The next morning, before continuing the trip, they stopped for breakfast at a local diner. Jonna needed to use the restroom which was outside the diner in a separate building. As she approached the bathroom, she stopped in her tracks and noticed a sign above the door, written in block letters, the sign said "whites only!"

Folks who lived in the north, above the Mason Dixon Line, certainly heard about the strong prejudices of those living in the southern states. To see it up close and personal was a different matter. Black people lowered their eyes when passing a white person and often moved to the other side of the street to avoid any contact whatsoever.

The next day they reached Jacksonville, the northernmost city in Florida, where they were greeted at a "welcome center." The center provided info about hotel/motels, sightseeing suggestions and most importantly, they offered fresh squeezed orange juice from fresh picked fruit right off the tree! Jonna thought that this must be paradise; the palm trees swayed in a gentle breeze, the wonderfully groomed surroundings were lush with verdant growth; ripe coconuts dropped to the ground from their high clusters in the trees.

Route 1 is a byway that hugs the eastern coast, along the Atlantic Ocean stretching from Maine to Florida, interrupted by some detours to A1A and other alternate connecting routes. They passed all the coastal towns and cities in Florida and finally arrived in South Miami along Collins Avenue.

The movie set for "A Hole in the Head" was filmed at the Cordoza Hotel, renamed in the movie, "Garden of Eden." Naturally, Marie took a room in that hotel for the duration of their stay. The room was stuffy, with no air-conditioning; it had 2 single beds and a cot for Jonna and Minnie. But hey, they walked the same halls and stood in the same lobby as Old Blue Eyes himself. For Marie, it didn't get much better than that. Across the street from the hotel was a stone wall that ran a good way between the hotel and the beach. Supposedly, Frank and Eddie sang the song High Hopes on that wall. Marie and Jonna did likewise.

Grandma accompanied Marie and Jonna, with Minnie in tow, to scout out the area around the Fontainbleau Hotel situated a ways up on the beach where the expensive hotels were. The hotel was famous for having hosted many celebrities and at some time the man himself... Frank Sinatra. There was a lounge on the first level of the hotel where photos of Frank with other prominent people were displayed. They took seats at the bar, ordered drinks, and began drilling the bartender about what it was like to serve Mr. Sinatra.

After strolling around the gardens of the luxury hotel, they picked up some take-out for dinner and returned to the Cordoza. If Jonna remembers correctly, the cost of the room was about $4.00 a night and did have a bathroom in the room.

To suggest that Marie was obsessed with the entertainer is surely an understatement. The word "worship" comes to mind. Undoubtedly, Frank was a very talented performer who rose to fame during the 1940's that lasted for several decades into the 1980's. He was nominated for and won an academy award for his portrayal of Maggio in the movie "From Here to Eternity." His possible involvement with the "mob" is legendary and probably has some truth to it.

His hundreds of recordings, albums, shows and movies live on in the minds and hearts of his faithful followers to the present day, those who are still alive anyway.

Teenage Years
Part One

Liberation for Jonna came when she was 16 years old. After attending Walton High School for a year and a half, the school allowed her to drop out. Marie filled out the necessary paperwork and Jonna was released from attending school. The time she spent at the school was horrible for her and she often skipped school claiming she felt ill with migraine headaches. She didn't have migraine headaches at all, but it was a good excuse.

The classroom atmosphere was a bit chaotic, the students undisciplined; a difficult environment for learning. In addition Jonna was regularly bullied by the other girls because she was different, a goody two shoes, so to speak. Jonna wasn't a joiner anyway and didn't even relate to the nerd cliques. The movie "Grease" highlighted the customs and lifestyles of the mainstream thinking of high school kids during the mid to late 1950s and into the 60's. Jonna just didn't fit in.

Marie found a secretarial school on Fordham Road and enrolled Jonna in a 6-month program to prepare her for the work force. The school taught, among other things, typing and steno. Remember there was very little automation at the time so Jonna gained proficiency on a manual typewriter and was able to type 60 words a minute accurately. She took the course in Gregg steno and was able to take dictation at 90 words a minute. With some prepping to look older, and armed with these skills, Jonna felt ready to enter the work force and combed the want ads in the local newspapers.

However, she applied for a job where these acquired skills were unnecessary. She answered an ad to work in a photo studio, for a job doing something she had never heard of before. Although she was nervous during the interview, she carried it off somehow and was hired.

The studio was located on McLean Avenue in Yonkers. They took family and individual portrait photos both in the home and at the studio. Fortunately they provided training and Jonna quickly picked up the skills for this relatively easy job. The job title was called a "Spotter." It involved using a graphite pencil to fill in the white spots that appeared in black and white photos printed on a semi-smooth photo paper stock. Sometimes she was allowed to watch the developing process in the dark room. The studio paid $1.00 an hour for a 40-hour workweek (9-5) with a paid hour for lunch. It felt like a fortune for the 16 year-old Jonna!

Strangely enough, Jonna was honored to contribute financially to the family. Marie felt that Jonna could keep $10.00 out of her paycheck for spending money; the remainder went into the family budget to run the household.

As you might suspect, Marie had a job a few doors down on McLean Avenue working for a construction company. This arrangement worked out very well because they could drive to and from work together. Marie worked the same hours.

These types of jobs were not career track by any stretch of the imagination, but represented a modest income to supplement Grandma's Social Security. After six-months of employment, Marie was let go, for some unknown reason, and she applied for Unemployment Insurance.

Jonna left the job at the photo studio as well since traveling to and from work was difficult as using public transportation required 2 bus changes.

Jonna accompanied Marie to the Unemployment Office, also located in the Fordham Road area. That turned out to be a very interesting experience for Jonna. After applying for the benefits, the applicant was given a folded card with printed columns to record dates of job interviews and the contact person and the dates. Also there was a column for the letter-writing applications one sent out during the week. If she remembers correctly, 6 possible jobs in your field of employment had to be contacted. In this case, Marie was able to go on for several months without finding a suitable job.

In the meantime, Jonna found temporary jobs at a few companies located on the Bronx/Yonkers border including, Mount Vernon. She was able to take busses to and from work.

Jonna loved to work. It was an outlet from the daily household routine and she interacted well with older people and bosses. The experience acquired during the workdays prepared her for future more well-paying jobs and the extra money was great. She was able to buy her own clothes in addition to the ones she sewed herself.

Wow! She really felt grown-up as the seeds of independence took root and blossomed.

Teenage years
Part Two

By most standards, Jonna did not have the usual teenage growing up experiences. Rather she was ushered into Marie's world when she was quite young. Whether growing up under Marie's tutelage was healthy or not would remain to be seen.

When Jonna was around 17 years old, Cousin Bea teamed up with Marie and Jonna and formed the "dynamic trio." They cavorted from club to club, bar to bar, and racetrack to racetrack. Most Friday evenings were spent at Yonkers Raceway where the trotters and pacers ran from the spring to the fall.

Before going into the track, the threesome met one of Marie's admirers, who they dubbed the name "big Charlie." Charlie was about 6'4" and looked, to Jonna, like a cowboy. He wore a ten-gallon white hat, a bolo tie, and shiny cowboy boots. The group met Charlie at a lounge across the street from the track. Charlie took a shine to Marie and became a sort of boyfriend. He treated the threesome to dinner and drinks before heading over to the track.

Technically, Jonna was underage to enter the track, but met with no questions or delays as she moved along with the crowd. At one of the concession stands in the middle of the partially enclosed better's area was another guy named Charlie, who became friendly with Marie, Bea and Jonna. Marie called him "little Charlie" because he was diminutive and skinny.

Once in a while, Marie invited little Charlie and a couple of the truckers over for drinks after work. Marie's job included dispatching truckers to various pick-up and drop off locations throughout the midwest and into the east. When they were in town, they had a standing invite.

Marie served Jack Daniels neat and/or with soda. Needless to say that was Frank Sinatra's drink of choice.

During those years, Marie's abdominal pain became more regular and the booze seemed to reduce the pain somewhat, at least that's what she told Jonna.

The record player was smoking with the latest Frank Sinatra album. Marie went so far as to decorate the living room wall with the album covers in a neat row, with cut out letters above spelling out Frank Sinatra followed by two or three exclamation points! The obsession was alive and well.

Other evenings were spent at clubs in the city featuring performers like Buddy Rich, a fading drummer, and, of course, Errol Gardner, a world renowned stylized pianist with his unique sound. It was said that Errol could not read music, but played by another sense sometimes called playing by ear. He produced his own rendition of popular tunes in haltingly syncopated style while humming along with the music. Sometimes Marie would get up on stage and sing one of the standards of earlier days. She had a good voice, and sounded professional.

Her desire to get Jonna into show business and become a performer was undaunted by the fact that Jonna couldn't even carry a tune!

Somehow she found out about a "cattle call" for girls to audition for the chorus line at the world famous Copa Cabana. The Copa was a distinct nightclub that booked famous entertainers for their review and drew a crowd willing to pay top dollar for dinner and the show.

Jonna donned on her black leotard, fishnet stockings and the highest heels she could find and got ready to stand in line with the other girls. A group of 6 girls were called to stand in a line and be either selected or dismissed. Her heart was in her throat as she gingerly walked on stage to be examined. She looked like a peanut compared to the other regular chorus girls. These girls had long legs and stood at least 8 inches taller than Jonna. Needless to say, she didn't make the cut and walked off stage with a feeling of rejection.

Jonna did not have aspirations to be in show business in any form. She thought that it was too tough a lifestyle and shied away from the limelight anyway. Her interests lie elsewhere.

Leather Making

They were always busy with something. Jonna grew up surrounded by the adventure of learning how to craft, sew, crochet, knit, paint, cook, and other creative endeavors.

Most evenings there was a project to be worked on or something to finish. Marie became enthused about working with leather. Up on Gun Hill Road, there was a shop that sold handmade leather goods of all sorts, including purses, belts, handbags and slings along with tooled leather items, soft moccasins and braided adornment with a western flair. The shop smelled of dyed, cured and tanned animal skins and was very appealing to Jonna's senses. She thought of saddles and cowboy chaps, horse whips and western gear. All imagined, because she had never been anywhere near the west beyond the frontier of New Jersey!

The owner and craftsman of the shop was a tall, gangly guy with a distracting, bobbing Adams apple in his pale skinny neck. His name was Albee and he produced some high-quality and well-crafted items sold in his shop. Marie and Jonna found out that he was willing to sell them some skins and hides, such as goat, cow, vicuna and other exotic critters. Reluctantly, he sold pieces of these hides to Marie and gave some basic instruction about cutting, piecing and sewing the skins. They were told that cowhide was quite thick and how it was sliced into several layers of skins that produced suede, and other soft leathers, and how top grain cowhide was often used for expensive furniture and other custom-made items. Most of the commercially mass-produced handbags, especially the patched sewn and pieced together hobo bags, were scraps of inferior quality leather.

Once introduced to this craft Marie and Jonna's interest took off. They eagerly began to pursue the art of leather crafting. In addition to the local shop, they made semi-monthly trips into the city to purchase tooling and cutting instruments along with hole punchers of different sizes and special needles and thread to penetrate the tough leather. The store attendants helped with some instruction to complete a project and produce a finished piece.

They went at it full swing for several months leading into the Christmas season. On one of the trips to Staten Island, they brought several completed pieces, like handbags and purses, and sold them to Marie's cousins who appreciated the low-cost and well-made items.

As the months progressed and more skill acquired, Marie came up with yet another scheme and decided to make several gifts for the Sinatra family. Frank Sinatra's mother, nicknamed "Dolly," still lived in their family home in Hoboken, New Jersey.

Every evening Marie and Jonna labored to produce several gifts to present at the forthcoming meeting. A Vicuna wallet for Frank, a purse for his Mama and Jonna crocheted a double loop entryway throw rug. It took a couple of weeks to get these gifts together and formulate a convincing story.

Marie came up with a somewhat plausible story that her mother, Carmela Lancona, had met Mrs. Sinatra at a Democratic meeting back in the early 1940's. Grandpa Al was active in the Democratic Party at the time. Marie conjured up a tale that they had met and formed a casual acquaintance during those years. Marie said that her mother was reminiscing one day about the "old days" and the memories of those she knew way back when.

Dolly Sinatra had been a diplomat from the old days in the Party. It was reported that she had "a politician's temperament, restless, energetic, unreflective." She earned the respect of the local politicians who made her a Democratic ward leader. In 1919 she chained herself to city hall in support of the Women's Suffrage movement. She also worked as a midwife, earning $50.00 for each delivery, a fair amount of money in those days. She was a woman of standing in her own right, besides the fact that she mothered Frank, her only child who became a legend in his own time.

And so on Christmas Eve in 1959 they made the trip to Hoboken New Jersey. Mrs. Sinatra lived in a quiet old neighborhood on a seldom traveled street in the suburbs of Hoboken. It was a modest house and gave no indication that her famous and rich son was a one-time resident.

It was beginning to snow. Marie and Jonna approached the front door with their hearts in their throats. They had no idea about what kind of reception they would get. And so they rang the bell and waited. Shortly an elderly woman, certainly Dolly herself, answered the door. Marie made introductions by saying that she was sort of an emissary for her mother, Carmela. She produced a picture of Grandma from that time and showed it to Mrs. Sinatra and asked if she recalled the woman in the photo. Much to their combined surprise she said, "yes I do remember Carmela." Jonna thought that the aging woman was being polite and diplomatic just in case she really had met her in those days.

For some unknown reason, she welcomed these strangers with grace and thanked them for the lovely gifts. They in turn offered regards from Carmela and wished her a Merry Christmas.

They had pulled it off! Or did they? Who was playing who? They would never know.

The ground started to get slick from the steady snow as they made their way to a local pub in Hoboken overlooking the shimmering Manhattan skyline. They were celebrating and reveling in that they got so close to the Sinatra family.

It was nearing midnight when they finally arrived home, but sleep did not come easy to the impersonators. The planning and executing of the subterfuge was surely an exhilarating experience!

This story is only one of the many stories about how Marie tried to make the Sinatra connection. Marie connived her way along several avenues to meet "ole blue eyes" in person as the following chapters will reveal.

In retrospect, Jonna believes that she and Marie were living vicariously through the life and career of the famous celebrity nicknamed "the chairman of the board."

The 500 Club
Part I

WNEW, the popular radio station in the 1950s and 60's, was rife with information about the next Sinatra event. The disc jockey, William B. Williams, played the standards dating from the late 1940's. He chose current releases as well featuring artists like Doris Day, Nat King Cole, Jerry Vale and even some Presley and some of the better rock n roll.

During one of his early morning broadcasts, he announced an upcoming contest. The winners would get two front row tickets to the Frank Sinatra nightclub performance at the famous 500 Club in Atlantic City, New Jersey, and an introduction to Frank backstage. Three sets of 2 tickets were being offered, all entries to be received at the station 2 weeks before the performance date.

Skinny D'Amato owned and operated the well-attended club and booked top-of-the charts entertainers, those who would draw big crowds to a sell-out audience.

Many of the club owners in Atlantic City were connected so to speak. They knew people, who, knew other people in the circle of mob bosses and close associates. The Cosa Nostra (our thing) or Mafia members were mostly of Sicilian ancestry on one or both sides of their family and very active during the 1950 s and 60s with their hands in the entertainment business, gambling, prostitution, loan-sharking and the numbers rackets.

Frank himself was half Sicilian on his father's side; he hailed from Lercara Friddi, near Palermo. His mother, Natalina Garaveta, was from Genoa; Frank (Francis Albert Sinatra) was a first-generation United States born citizen of immigrant parents. Because of his ancestry, he may have been welcomed into the fold and given special status. We may never know the depth of his involvement with this nefarious group, and maybe it's better that way. His talent and charisma speak for themselves and that is what he is remembered for.

Marie began formulating an idea about how to get the free tickets. She wrote directly to William B. Williams at the radio station; a carefully worded letter requesting that her daughter Jonna meet with him personally and discuss the possibility of winning the tickets, she enclosed a current picture of Jonna. She claimed that the mother/daughter team were Sinatra fans from back in the days of the big bands and would be ecstatic if they won the drawing.

Much to their surprise, Willy B. replied and agreed to meet Jonna at a restaurant in Midtown Manhattan for lunch. Oh my goodness! The opportunity of a lifetime just opened up for Marie to get closer to the Sinatra scene.

After the luncheon meet was confirmed, Marie and Jonna set out to purchase an outfit appropriate enough for the occasion. The upscale clothing store, Best & Co., was located on the Post Road in Scarsdale in Westchester County which they frequented from time to time. On the first level of the store was a restaurant with a good selection of luncheon fare; quiche, muffins, coffee and salads were on the menu.

Marie loved that store. It might have been because at one time when her father was alive, she had spending money and could afford higher-end clothing and shoes. Nevertheless, at this stage in her life, most of the items were too pricey for her limited budget. Undeterred, she and Jonna shopped the sales and found real bargains in her dress size. They settled for a black two-piece suit in the Jackie Kennedy style popular at that time. It fit like a glove and looked stunning on Jonna. Coupled with some complimentary accessories, the bill came to around $75.00, a tidy sum for Marie's pocketbook. In 2020 that would equal about a whopping $782.00, a fairly pricey outfit.

Marie trimmed Jonna's hair into a chic, below the ear bob, that nicely framed her face. A touch of light makeup and manicured nails and she was ready to go! Marie prepped Jonna as to how to speak and act during this luncheon. Jonna was often put on the spot to act and behave older than her years, so she accepted this instruction with ease.

Jonna boarded the D train at 206th St. down to the city and emerged at the 59th street platform, smack dad in midtown Manhattan. She walked with an air of confidence, that maybe she might not have felt inside. The luncheon was set for 12:30 and hopefully Willy B. would be awaiting her arrival. The restaurant was crowded, but she spotted him sitting at a 2-top table in the center of the restaurant. He did not rise as Jonna approached and that set her off a bit. A gentlemen would have stood up to greet her.

Jonna introduced herself, they shook hands, and Jonna's butterflies eased up. After ordering and small chit chat, Jonna made her pitch. She told the disc jockey that her mother was in failing health and it would be the dream of a lifetime to see "ole blue eyes" in person, before she became more seriously ill. Was there any way they could find themselves winners of the great prize?

Jonna couldn't imagine what Willy B was thinking about her and her request. Did he expect sexual favors in payment for the tickets? That aside, he remained courteous, but told Jonna in no uncertain terms that they had to enter the contest and submit their entry as the thousands of others had done. He did offer to put their names in the drawing box and hope for the best. Special selection would be against the rules! Ouch! That really hurt! After all the prep and expense, she realized that her girlish wit and charm did nothing to sway the disc jockey. The luncheon ended cordially enough, although her disappointment must have been noticed.

On the way back uptown, she detoured a bit and took a stroll along Fifth Avenue and did some window shopping; she passed stores like Neiman Marcus, Tiffany's, Sachs and other high priced boutiques. This little jaunt on one of the most famous streets in the world made up for the disappointment in the outcome of her mission.

The 500 Club
Part II

Marie took the news very well. However, she immediately set in motion another plan to get down to Atlantic City and get tickets to the show the regular way. She made several phone calls and requests and finally secured 3 tickets for the Friday night show early in August. She sent a check for the tickets; there were no credit cards in regular use at that time. Probably only corporate, business or wealthy persons used Carte Blanche or American Express. The year was 1959 and Jonna was going to be 17 years old in November, still not of age to be nightclubbing!

With the reservations in place, the next step was to find a nice hotel within their budget and near the club. She finally chose the Claridge Hotel on Indiana Avenue. The streets in Atlantic City are named after states. They were assigned a room on an upper floor with a view of the ocean; the room also had a salt-water tub in the bathroom for soaking. It was a luxury they could afford for at least one night anyway.

The threesome left the Bronx on a Friday morning, took the Garden State Parkway down to the shore area and arrived at the hotel around check-in-time; they navigated their way using a printed paper map of New Jersey. There was plenty of time to primp and dress for the 10:00

pm show. Although the room had an upscale feel to it, Bea found a toenail clipping on the floor near her bed. Sheesh! They laughed about this and threatened to report the stray toenail to management, maybe they could get a discount?

Marie and Jonna brought along a portable record player for the trip; they had the latest Frank Sinatra album "Nice n Easy" playing on the turntable all afternoon while singing along and dancing around. They even brought the player to the beach where they hung out for a while soaking in a few rays. It was hot and humid and sandy, not all that enjoyable really.

Nearby there was a coffee shop that boasted that they served the largest cup of coffee in the nation! They drank the freshly brewed coffee from HUGE cups and killed some time awaiting their booked show time at the 500 Club. Time seemed to move slowly as their anticipation grew. The club offered 3 seating times, 10, 12, and 2 pm.

In the 1950's Atlantic City was the only legal and possibly illegal gambling center on the east coast. High rollers and chronic gamblers showed up en masse to push their luck at the tables and slots. Marie, Jonna and Bea were on a tight budget, pinching pennies, and didn't want to waste money, even on the penny slot machines.

They spent some time walking the boardwalk and out onto the famous Steel Pier which resembled older days when it was built in 1898 and touted to be "one of the most notable theme parks in the country."

Over the years, the Pier changed hands several times but still presented various acts and performers that appealed to wide audiences; it hosted thousands of entertainers, show biz personalities and circus acts. Big names like the Harry James Band, Dianna Ross, Dick Clark, the Rolling Stones, Ray Charles, Abbott and Costello, Frank Sinatra and several diving-horse acts.

The Steel Pier passed to Donald Trump when he took over Resorts in 1987. Located near the northern end of the boardwalk (opposite of what became the Trump Taj Mahal casino) its busy, frenetic atmosphere has been re-created by and starring some Soprano's alumni, set in a thinly fictionalized Prohibition-era Atlantic City.

Back at the hotel, they started getting ready to make their appearance. Make-up was carefully applied, hair teased, jewelry and specially purchased outfits donned; the three attractive ladies looked and felt confident in their appearance.

When they arrived at the club, at least an hour ahead of time, the queue was already 4 deep and at least a hundred feet long. The air was electric! They waited and waited when finally, the club doors opened and the first crowd was hustled in. After admitting about 500 people the doors closed, they were about 10 rows behind in line. They were told to wait for the 12:00 am show or return the following night; this was in spite of having confirmed reservations. By that time, they were bone tired, their feet ached, their make-up melting and their spirits low. They decided to return the following night.

Check-out time at the Claridge was noon. They woke up late that Saturday morning and trudged down to the lobby with suitcases in tow. With hours to kill before the night's performance they headed for the beach with small beach towels and tried to get more rest. The wind was blowing and whipped up the loose sand coating their bodies and hair with talcum-like deposits. They were sweaty and sticky by the end of the day and in no way presentable for the show.

The three Musketeers were adaptable and used the sinks in the public bathrooms to clean up. Some what clean, they returned to the car and attempted to get dressed in the close confines of the small Chevy. Putting on nylons, their evening clothes, doing makeup again. It was a comical scene and they laughed their way through a pretty funny situation. Queued up again, they were finally admitted to the 2:00 am and last show.

The ushers showed them to a table that seated about 10 people. They ordered a bottle of Jack Daniels; ice, soda and glasses were supplied to make your own drink. The crowd was psyched. Electricity filled the air. Faithful fans awaited their hero. Soon the house lights dimmed and Pat Henry, a well-known comedian, took the stage and warmed up the crowd with his contemporary humor.

Again, the house lights dimmed to almost complete darkness. The crowd was hushed. The master of ceremonies announced… and now ladies and gentlemen, the chairman of the board. After the cheers and hoots and hollars died down, a thin spotlight lit up Frank's face where he was already seated. He opened with his rendition of "Fly me to the moon." He sang many more of his well-known arrangements interspersed with some theatrical patter. At the end when he walked off stage the audience was on their feet calling for more, more, more! Frank returned to the stage and performed for another half an hour to please his fans.

The adorning crowd wandered out of the club around 4:30 in the wee small hours of the morning. (no pun intended). The sun was already coming up in the eastern sky. The whole experience was magical and the crowd was still mesmerized and glowing from the Sinatra magnetism. It was amazing! Marie, Bea and Jonna filed down the deserted street still glowing from the whole experience.

Jonna looks back to those days with nostalgia. They were special. She experienced a time in entertainment history that would never be duplicated in quite the same way, and rightly so; there was only one Frank Sinatra and his legacy lingers on.

18 and 19 years old

When we are young and energetic and full of enthusiasm for life, we think we can do anything and in most cases we do. Jonna survived the next few years operating on remote control. There was little time to think.

Marie was still functioning, although bouts with abdominal pain were more frequent, she was still able to work full-time. Jonna was also working full-time and combined with Grandma's SS they were managing quite well; they had some "disposable" income to spend.

One Friday evening, after work, they went to a club in Hoboken, New Jersey, situated on the palisades with a spectacular view of the Manhattan skyline, the one they went to after visiting with Mrs. Sinatra.

It had a congenial atmosphere and not considered to be a pick-up joint, but catered to the locals looking to have a few drinks after work and hang out with friends. The old colorful juke box played the current hits and oldies at a cost of 25 cents for 6 selections, the music never stopped. Jonna was in entertainment mode as she mimed the songs and danced around the bar.

A cute young man, kind of a Steve Macqueen look-alike, made the overture to strike up a conversation with Jonna. Jonna was flattered because most of the men who tried to make her acquaintance were older. He asked her what she was drinking and bought a round. He was decked out in a sailor's uniform and told Jonna he was in town on a shore leave from his ship. They chatted a while and Jonna gave him her phone number and address as he promised to keep in touch. All ended well that night and Marie and Jonna got back home around 1:00 am.

Grandma's health was in continual decline; she was very uncomfortable and moaned while pushing a chair up and down the hallway in the apartment toward her bedroom. A visit to the doctor revealed that she had an abdominal tumor that had to be removed. She was hospitalized, the operation performed, and returned home to resume moaning and pushing the chair. However, the tumor was benign, and she made a slow but steady recovery.

It wasn't long after Grandma's surgery that Marie also began to decline in health suffering more and more regular pain that disabled her for longer periods of time. She eventually was unable to hold down full-time or even part-time employment. Both she and Grandma were "down for the count" in so many words. The family now depended on Jonna's income to get by. She started to assume more of the household duties in addition to working full time.

One Saturday, out of the blue, a FFS delivery man showed up at the door with a long package, tied with a big colorful bow addressed to Miss Banderet. The package contained a dozen yellow roses nestled in a bed of green foliage and baby's breath. They were so pretty! Jonna felt like a queen. That feeling would end quite abruptly when Marie saw that the flowers were from "sailor boy." She proceeded to extract the flowers from the box, throw them on the floor, and stomp them with all her might until only a smashed pulpy mess remained; she cursed this boy out with every expletive imaginable and threw the flowers in the garbage. Jonna was stunned, embarrassed and hurt on many levels. She thought that Marie had lost her mind and blamed her illness for such erratic behavior. The message was loud and clear to Jonna, she was to have no boyfriends, suitors, dates or whatever even though she was almost 18 years old.

Jonna had been working for a Real Estate Management Company located in the Wagner Building. The job came to an abrupt end, when they moved their offices to Manhattan. To continue working there, Jonna would have to ride the subway into the city five days a week. She did not take well to the new arrangement and quit the job.

The daily routine of caring for two ailing people was tiring and depressing; she wanted to get back to work, at least that would be some relief from the drudgery.

It is difficult to describe what young Jonna was going through. She had no life of her own, no friends, no personal ideas, and didn't make any personal choices about her future. Even if she did have choices, she didn't know what they were. The whirlwind of activity kept her focused on the needs of her mother and grandmother to the exclusion of anything she might want to pursue. Forget about going to school or developing another lifestyle. She was bound by some unspoken duty, the attitude of which was a remnant from older days when children sacrificed for the welfare of other family members. To do otherwise would be reproachful and shameful and out of line. There was no one else to pick up the reins and steer the horse. She was it.

Time Passages

Jonna was far away from her God. She didn't think God had anything to do with her circumstances and by the same token she didn't think God would intervene and show her a correct path. She believed she was on her own and able to make reasonable decisions by herself; she didn't pray but moved headlong into the next phase that life presented. Maybe if she took the time to step back and do some thinking about what was best for her things might have turned out different. She would never know.

Once again, Jonna scoured the local want ads for a suitable job. She highlighted one ad seeking a secretary working for an attorney in White Plains. No salary was listed but that it would depend on the training and experience of the applicant. She called the number and set up an interview.

The bus ride from the Woodlawn bus stop took about 35 minutes. She was dropped off in the middle of White Plains and found the building where the interview would take place. She immediately liked the atmosphere; the entryway and hallways leading up to several professional offices were tidy and well maintained.

Jonna interviewed well; she presented a home-made resume highlighting her training and previous jobs, a bit embellished perhaps, but mostly accurate. The attorney said he had a few more interviews lined up and would make a decision by the end of the week. Jonna held her breath and waited.

Somewhat to her surprise, the attorney did call on Thursday of that same week and offered a starting salary of $75.00 and asked if she would begin on the following Monday at 9:00 am. She eagerly accepted and prepared to start a new career, as an assistant, in the field of law! After deductions and travel and expenses, Jonna could bring home a clear $50.00 a week and add to the family income.

Meanwhile, Marie's illness took starts and stops, resembling 2 steps forward and 3 steps backward. Grandma wasn't in much better shape and both seemed to be crawling for survival.

After that first week of work, when Saturday rolled around, Jonna loaded Marie and their dog "Shep" (a full-blooded German Shepherd) into the Chevy for a day trip up to Phoenicia. Marie was feeling pretty well that day and they spent a few hours picnicking and strolling around near the brook; she took a few pictures for the memory album.

The New York State Thruway was completed in this section and Jonna cruised along going the speed limit. When she glanced up in the rear-view mirror, a police car was tailing her with flashing lights. She gingerly pulled over to the side of the road. The officer approached. He asked to see her driver's license and registration. Jonna was puzzled by this pull over, after all she was not exceeding the speed limit.

As she extracted the license and registration from its holder, a piece of military script she had been given as a souvenir, was caught by a breeze and blew down the road behind the car. The officer made an attempt to retrieve the money, but the wind took it away too fast. Jonna said not to worry, that it was just military script and of no value. She then asked the officer why she was being stopped. He pointed out that she was tailgating in the left lane. The left lane was for passing only and she needed to remain in the right lane until the opportunity to pass was safe. He acknowledged that she was a new driver and only gave her a warning ticket. She learned a valuable lesson that day…. Stay out of the left lane unless you are passing a slower moving car!

Jonna was enjoying her job working for the attorney. Most of the dictation she took was easy enough to transcribe and all other documents were boilerplate fill ins on the word processor. One morning, a young man knocked on the open door and said hello; he had an office right next door. They introduced themselves and struck up a casual conversation. His name was Paul, not especially handsome, but a nice-enough fellow nonetheless with a likeable personality. He was the manager and chief cook and bottle washer for the company Carriet Messenger Service. The owner had turned the business decisions and functions over to Paul; he essentially ran the business. He operated a delivery service in White Plains and other nearby Westchester locations. IBM was one of the main customers. These were the days when local deliveries, including letters and packages, were hand delivered by messenger services to and from various locations. It represented a decent living for Paul with the opportunity of taking over the company in time. He also made a lot of contacts that would serve him well in the future. Everybody liked Paul; he had an easy-going and affable personality. He was a good listener and had a knack of sizing up people rather quickly. So along with his natural business savvy, he steadily moved into the broader business world.

He brought breakfast in most mornings and they shared coffee and rye toast and cream cheese, Paul's favorite. A few times they went to lunch together and soon he drove Jonna home pretty regularly. I guess these occasions would be called "dates." Jonna asked him if he was Italian. He said "no" that he was Jewish and did that matter. It didn't necessarily matter to Jonna, but she instinctively knew that Marie would not be happy with this information.

Although they never really talked about it, Paul respected Jonna's position about a sexual relationship, since her upbringing forbade pre-marital or promiscuous sex in any form; however, he was patient and bided his time, a strategic move on his part. Jonna was a plum ripe for the picking, but that would have to wait

Marie and Jonna at Sprain Brook Parkway.

Jonna posing for dance portfolio, 1962.

Grandma in front of Cordozo Hotel. Miami Beach

Grandma, Marie, Marguerite. Cross County Shopping Center.

Jonna graduation from Junior High.

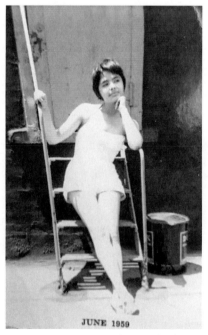

JUNE 1959

Jonna up on the roof.

Part IV

Changes in the Wind

One afternoon, Jonna's mother, Marie doubled over with excruciating pain in her abdomen. There was only one choice for Jonna and that was to get Marie into the Chevy and ride up the few blocks to Montefiore Hospital emergency entrance. She was immediately put on a stretcher and wheeled away in haste to the operating room. The harried nurses wheeled her toward the emergency room; the doctor unhesitatingly performed emergency surgery. It took a few hours of patiently waiting for the operating doctor to emerge with a somewhat grim look on his face. Marie was alive and made it through the operation, but the grapefruit-size tumor on her ovary burst during the procedure, spreading cancer spores throughout her abdomen. They were able to clean up most of the cancer cells, but it was impossible to get it all.

He announced that the emergency surgery saved her life for now, but that treatment would follow after her recovery. Jonna was not given a prognosis and was in the dark about what the future would hold for Marie. The "C" word was avoided; there was hope for her future. At that time in 1962 there was no chemo therapy but only radiation treatment that commenced in a couple of weeks. She was also given pain medication and sent home to convalesce.

Marie was managing fairly well for a few months and able to get to the hospital for treatment by herself. She even drove the car and did some shopping and things were looking up. Grandma was able to do some cooking and the household atmosphere wasn't quite as grim. Jonna was still working and still keeping up with the other chores and responsibilities that awaited her daily.

In the meantime, Paul stopped by to pick-up Jonna a couple of evenings during the week. She was introduced to some of Paul's friends and then to Rachel, Paul's mother. They lived in a quiet neighborhood off the Boston Post Road on Corsa Avenue in the east Bronx. She was a lovely lady who dressed nicely, wore expensive jewelry, and primped up daily. Rae was about 4'10" inches tall. To help heighten her diminutive appearance, she wore very high heel shoes: her hair was dyed a bright red and teased up, as was the common style of the day.

Paul indicated that he and Jonna were becoming serious. Rae said "she's a lovely girl, but couldn't you find a nice Jewish girl?"

Jonna began to think that her rescue was at hand and had a sort of worshipful attitude toward Paul. She had no idea that the great escape from one situation would produce another more complex situation that would unfold rather quickly and unexpectantly. Jonna was totally unprepared for what the next few years would bring.

A friend once told Jonna about how happenstance events could alter the direction of one's life, beyond personal choices. For instance, "I met a man at a party who wore a red tie. And that's why I became a professor." What? Jonna began to wonder how many casual and seemingly unimportant experiences influenced her choices especially at a very young age.

Caught between a rock and a hard place, Jonna went ahead and agreed to get married. If given some other viable choices, marriage, a family and all that it entailed would be on the bottom of the list. She was stumbling along blindly and took what looked like an easy way out. Unfortunately, that choice would have an even more devastating effect on Jonna's somewhat naive and optimistic heart. She sold her soul to the Devil.

The Next Phase

Jonna bit the bullet and with much trepidation invited Paul to meet Marie and Grandma. Jonna felt that she might receive some kind of ok from Marie. She was dead wrong.

Paul knocked on the door and was let into the inquisitor's den. Jonna was on pins and needles, but Paul was his usual confident self and managed to get through the interview. Marie didn't like him right off the bat simply because he was a man and threatened to take her Jonna away and introduce her to another life.

You could cut the tension in the air with a dull knife. Grandma, composed as always, had little input. Marie's attitude was confrontational to say the least and clearly would not give her permission for Jonna to marry this less-than-satisfactory suitor. She told Jonna that she would not be welcomed back in the house if she went ahead with this absurd notion. The discussion ended and Paul left.

Immediately afterward, Uncle Jerry was called and asked to meet with Jonna for another third degree. She went to her uncle's apartment and had another sit-down. He let Jonna talk and soon realized that Jonna had made up her mind and no amount of further conversation was necessary. She had been taken in by Paul's attention and charisma. But just like a scorpion, the backlash sting would prove devastating in short order.

To illustrate how vehemently opposed Marie was to this possible marriage, she inquired, through some contacts, how she could "put out a contract" to have Paul eliminated. Jonna found out about this threat through the grapevine and alerted Paul that this ridiculous threat might become reality. Paul realized that Marie was probably off her rocker but still took the threat seriously. He took some precautions to protect himself.

The invisible underworld contact proposed that the job could be done at a cost of $2500.00. Even with whatever funds Marie could beg borrow or steal, she couldn't get together that absurd amount of money. And to think that was the bargain price!

What a mess. Jonna stayed away from Paul for a while and only met him in the evening on a few occasions. They knew each other for just over three months and officially dated about a dozen or so times. Albeit a very short courtship for two strangers, the ball was on the court and rolling steadily toward a marriage.

If Jonna and Paul were not put into this pressure cooker of a situation, things might have been different. They could have dated for a longer period of time, got to know each other better and made more reasonable plans, if any at all. But it was not to be.

Marie finally abandoned the quest to have Paul "rubbed out" and settled down a bit. Life at home went on. She continued the weekly treatments and it was obvious that she was in a steady decline. She was an angry, discontented woman feeling that she failed with Jonna. How terribly sad for all concerned.

Sadie, Sadie Married Lady

Jonna had given notice to her boss in White Plains that she was getting married and would be resigning from the job.

Paul picked Jonna up from the apartment in the evening of April 9th, 1963. She had some clothing put together in a small suitcase in preparation for leaving the house and starting a new life. He was driving a panel truck that had no treads on the gas pedal or brake. They drove around for a while and wound up at an apartment that Paul and his friends kept for entertaining women; it was sort of a bachelor pad that he kept even after their marriage; they called the apartment the ranch

Jonna did think this arrangement was strange, but dismissed her thoughts figuring that she had no idea how men behaved anyway and this was probably quite normal.

Paul thought that Jonna should give intercourse a try, since they were getting married the next day anyway. She said ok and they proceeded to have the sexual union. It was a pretty uncomfortable experience and hurt a lot; Jonna noticed blood on her clothing. She couldn't figure out what all the talk about the glories of sex was referring to. Is this what Marie was saving her from? Not much fun or excitement and she thought that she may get better with the situation in time.

The following morning, they got dressed and went to Mount Vernon for the civil marriage ceremony. Larry Feather and Ira Circle were witnesses and it was over very quickly. They all went to a Chinese restaurant for a little congratulatory luncheon.

Afterward, they went back to Paul's mother's house where Rae awaited their arrival. They were given the large bedroom upstairs with an adjoining bath. The house was very fancy in Jonna's mind, with wall-to-wall dark green carpeting throughout and expensive looking furniture and drapery. It would be her place for only a short while.

Paul arranged for a honeymoon vacation in the Virgin Islands and Puerto Rico. He presented Jonna with a diamond wedding ring with a matching emerald cut diamond engagement ring. That was impressive to Jonna and thought that it sealed the marriage officially. Unfortunately, after several months Jonna had to give the ring back to Paul, he said it would be put away in a safe for safekeeping? Actually, the ring was reported stolen and the insurance company paid for the loss.

Rae was a terrific lady and made a pretty nice mother-in-law. She doted on Paul, since he was her favorite. Paul's older sister and brother were already married and out of the house. Dorothy was married to Sy. She had three children and was a school teacher, they lived in Connecticut; Paul nicknamed her Toddles. Irwin, nicknamed Iggy, was also married with two children and lived in Yonkers. Iggy, being Iggy in his crude manner, asked Jonna if she was an Indian, like Native American Indian? Since she had long straight dark hair she was often mistaken for Spanish, or Italian or sometimes Greek, but not often Indian!

Paul introduced Jonna to his circle of friends and family alike. There were a few get-togethers with food and drink and gifts to celebrate their marriage. It seemed to Jonna that they were an overly huggy, kissy kind of group which she was unaccustomed to; her family did not display affection in that manner. As Jonna recalls her time at home, they never even said "I love you" and hugging and kissing were out of the question. So very different.

She was at Rae's house for only a month or so, when Paul told Jonna that Marie had late-stage cancer and would was given about a year to live. After receiving this news, Jonna knew what she had to do. She visited Marie and Grandma several times a week, assisting, cleaning, helping in any way she could and stayed over some nights to be more available. Marie had to get to the hospital once a week for radiation treatment and renewed medication; Jonna was trying her best to be a caregiver and a wife.

Paul was patient with the situation and gave Jonna latitude to proceed as she saw fit given the circumstances. After a short while, Jonna realized that in essence, she was separated from Paul and saw him on fewer occasions and was confused as to where her loyalties should lie.

With all this confusion in mind, Jonna decided to get an apartment a few blocks away, on the other side of Gun Hill Road. It was a studio and within walking distance from Marie and Grandma's apartment. At least Paul could move in with her and they would share some sort of a married relationship.

She continued to visit Marie about three times a week and took care of necessary chores. Marie continued to rally with some good days, some better days and worse days.

Don't Blink

Was Jonna ready? I don't think so. After being married for only a few months, she became pregnant. The first sign of this phenomena was that Jonna felt nauseous at the thought of drinking coffee; another sign was a missed period and feeling out of sorts.

She was recommended to see a gynecologist group in Bronxville that touted pain free delivery as their specialty. That sounded good. On her first appointment she was seen by Dr. Lawrence where he pronounced her a healthy specimen and certainly able to deliver a baby with no problems. The due date was March 17th of the following year (1964).

Paul was concerned that Jonna had too much on her plate and may not have been mentally or emotionally ready to assume more responsibility by having this baby. He asked her if she wanted to get an abortion and wait for a later time to get pregnant again. He knew people who could take care of this. Jonna was shocked at first and didn't know what to think. Although this pregnancy was unexpected by any stretch of the imagination, she wasn't ready to consider having an abortion. Even though she had barely adjusted to the fact that Marie would soon die, and that she was newly married, and that Grandma would still need care, that she lived away from home for the first time and that Paul was oftentimes not around. Holy smokes! A weaker individual would have caved, but Jonna believed she could do it all and do it all well enough.

Marie was also very upset, but not for the same reasons; she thought that bringing a child into the world would ruin Jonna's life. And to bring that "Jew bastard's" son into the world would be a big mistake for her. She seemed to know that the child would be a boy.

That next week Marie put the pressure on Jonna to accompany her to an adoption agency in White Plains to seek counseling and the possibility of putting the newborn up for adoption. It may seem absurd to think that Marie would go to those lengths to get rid of the child.

The interview went quickly when the woman interviewer heard that Jonna was legally married, and that the child had a father willing to assume the responsibility of raising the baby. Talk about an embarrassing situation for Jonna. Who in their right mind would even consider anything else except to deliver the baby and keep it; it was crazy on many levels.

The two most important people in her life were giving her not only poor advice, but destructive advice; she was in an emotional state, torn in all directions and seeking to please everyone in this decision.

The counselor told her to wait a while, deliver the baby, and then reconsider the decision. Of course, Paul would have to sign off on this adoption since he was the father. In her mind Jonna immediately dismissed any option but to go ahead and have the baby and of course keep it. What a freaking mess! She had no one to turn to. An average young girl, facing this situation, might have had a breakdown. Maybe Jonna was damaged on the inside, but outwardly carried on like she knew what she was doing. The weight of the situation was pressing in on all sides.

Finally, Marie gave in and accepted the fact that she was to become a grandmother in 6 months. She told Jonna that she didn't want to be called Grandma, but that she would be known to the baby as Marie.

Never Give Up

Marie was not about to give up or give in. She had a contact, through Dominic, who agreed to set-up a meeting of sorts at Jilly's restaurant in the city. He was Frank Sinatra's chauffer.

This chauffer, lets call him Tony, whispered in Sinatra's ear that Marie, a long-time fan, was well into the latter stages of cancer and her dream was to shake Frank's hand. Sinatra, known to be moved by compassion for individuals in need, agreed to meet Marie and Jonna at the restaurant located on W. 52nd Street.

When Frank was in New York, he frequented Jilly's accompanied by his close friends, other famous entertainers, and hangers-on. It has been reported that Jilly Rizzo was one of Frank's best friends. Frank apparently slept into the afternoon and would call up Jilly to alert him that he was to show up after 3:00 in the afternoon. Jilly responded by clearing a table and alerting the chef that the Chairman of the Board was due to arrive. His preferred meal was prepared, breaded veal cutlets with pasta and red sauce, and awaited his arrival. Frank was raised as an only child and vowed to always have people around him in his life; in his celebrity years he hung out with other famous people including the Kennedy's; he was part of the President's inner circle.

Marie and Jonna arrived around 3:00 pm and sat at the famous bar.

Marie didn't look that ill yet and with make-up her appearance was acceptable. Jonna wore a loose fitting silvery long sleeve blouse she bought for the occasion. At that time, she was about 4 months into her pregnancy and was beginning to show a slight baby bump that thickened her waist. The blouse was a poor disguise, but Marie still had delusions that Sinatra would spot Jonna and offer the young beauty (as Marie saw Jonna) a movie audition or some other form of introduction into show business.

Shortly after ordering drinks, the man himself showed up. Frank exited his limo parked right outside the restaurant followed by his chauffer Tony, who would make the introductions. He was handsome and well dressed in his usual cocked fedora, suit and tie for which he was famous. He approached Marie and shook her hand and said he was pleased to meet her. He turned to Jonna and said "hi kid" but didn't shake her hand. Was that it? Hi kid? Oh well, Jonna figured that was as good as it got in the presence of royalty! A throng of friends awaited his arrival as their private party revved up in the rear of the restaurant. It was interesting to see the convivial group of the rich and famous enjoying the privileges of their wealth and fame.

Jonna had to use the restroom, located in the rear part of the restaurant, and passed the noisy table. Marie was watching from the bar and reported that Frank gave Jonna more than a glance. She reasoned that he was impressed by her lovely daughter.

Marie had gotten her wish. Although Frank did not propose marriage to Jonna on the spot, she was content enough just to be in his immediate presence and enjoy the magnetism of his persona.

JFK

Marie and Jonna were shopping at Gimbels Department store in the Cross County Shopping Center in Yonkers. They went there a couple of times a month to peruse the stores and have lunch at the Gimbels café located on the third floor. Jonna picked up a couple of old-fashioned maternity tops like Lucy wore on the I Love Lucy Show when she was pregnant with Desi Junior; her belly was getting bigger by the week.

It was early afternoon when an announcement came over the loud speaker in the store. It said something like the President of the United States, John Fitzgerald Kennedy, was shot in Dallas, Texas; the details of this fatal shooting were not available at that time. The date was November 22, 1963.

After they got home and turned on the TV, it was confirmed that he, in fact, had been assassinated; the theories about why, and who did the shooting began to circulate. At 2:15 p.m., Lee Harvey Oswald, a new employee of the book depository, was arrested for JFK's assassination, as well as for the fatal 1:15 p.m. shooting of Dallas patrolman J.D. Tippit. Two days later on Nov 24, Oswald would be murdered by local nightclub owner and police informant, Jack Ruby, at point-blank range and on live TV.

For the next three days, the networks aired the continuing procession of the funeral; world leaders and dignitaries showed up for the services, including many show-business celebrities among the 800,000 mourners lining Pennsylvania Avenue. The sight of the toddler, John Jr., saluting as his father's 4-horse drawn caisson including a riderless black horse named Black Jack, moved slowly toward the church, brought viewers to tears. The famous headline photo shows Jackie, in a black designer outfit and veil, surrounded by family, including the actor Peter Lawford, who was married to Kennedy's sister and her two young children, Caroline and John, a mere toddler. Although all presidents have enemies, JFK seemed to be one of the most loved presidents to that date. He and his family, along with the elegant Jackie his wife, were revered and elevated to the level of royalty. He was the 35th president of the United States.

All branches of military service were represented in force, with traditional 21-gun salute, cannon shots, marching bands, the playing of taps and the folding of the American flag that draped the coffin and then presented to his widow. It was terribly moving and emotional to witness the whole proceeding on live television. Marie, Jonna and Grandma were glued to the tv for the duration. As far as Jonna remembers, all tv stations carried the most current developments of the event for the four-day vigil when Kennedy was finally laid to rest in Arlington National Cemetery. He was 46 years old and, also of note, the first Roman Catholic to hold the presidential office in the US.

Conspiracy theories about the assassination continued over the following years about the single bullet theory and other controversial aspects of the events. Many believed the government was withholding critical information. To this day, as of the writing of this memoire, analysts and other researchers continue the debate about the motivation for the assassination, the smoking gun, and other disputable reports.

They say that Americans have short memories and maybe that is true.

Certainly, the current generation has no personal recollection of those events and even the tragedy of 9/11 is far removed from their thoughts. For those of us who were alive and adult when these history-making events occurred, our vision may be a bit clouded about the details, but we will never forget.

1963-1964

The days and weeks seemed to disappear; there was always so much to do and not much time for reflection.

Jonna's treadmill activities included attending to Marie and Grandma, cleaning, cooking, hospital visits, and generally administering two households. Her belly was getting bigger, but she still managed to care for everything in her charge.

Thank goodness for youth! Although Jonna was young and inexperienced in a worldly sense, she was quite competent handling the domestic issues presented to her. Paul was missing in action as they say; he rarely made it home for dinner and was generally out of touch with Jonna's daily routine and responsibilities. They never had any kind of meaningful conversation or communication; they truly were on different planes of consciousness. Jonna supposed that he was very occupied with business, which she came to find out also included some "funny business." When Paul told Jonna that she was "one in a million" she didn't take it literally and supposed that he meant that she was special. What a joke! The joke was on Jonna.

Jonna's birthday, November 9th, Thanksgiving, Christmas and New Year's flew by in a flurry without much notice. There were more important things to take care of and little time for celebrating. Marie was in a decline; she wasn't able to do very much for herself any longer and Jonna picked up the slack. She helped with showers as Marie balked that the water spray was hurting her skin. By this time her skin was turning different colors within weeks. First, she looked jaundiced, then pale and then her wrinkled skin turned brown. There was no flesh or muscle beneath the skin and her limbs were very skinny, only her abdomen was bloated looking. Jonna's cousins, Bea, Gerald and Dennis showed up intermittently to lent a hand; any help was welcomed.

One morning in mid-March, Jonna started to feel some cramping in her lower abdomen. At first this squeezing feeling was half an hour apart for quite a while. The feeling began to come more often, like 15 minutes apart and soon it was 10 minutes apart. It was March 17th and the city was celebrating St. Patrick's Day.

St. Patrick's Day parade in New York City is the oldest and largest parade in the world and has marched on the streets of the city every year since 1762, fourteen years before the Declaration of Independence that established the United States. The parade was replete with bag pipers in traditional Irish garb, marching bands, cheerleaders with twirling batons, and club groups with banners, and groups of step dancers. Catholic schools were represented, city officials and Cardinals officiated and other celebrities who turned out for the festivities. The pubs and bars along the parade rounds spilled over with celebrants wearing green top hats, shamrocks and drinking a hearty Irish brew, Guinness dark beer. Jonna's cousin Bea marched in the parade for a few years in a row, representing St. Brenan's Church and School. St Patrick's Cathedral overflowed with reverent worshippers and tourists alike. Everyone got in the spirit and celebrated along with their Irish friends and relatives. Aunt Marge, Bea's mother, (Margaret MacNamara) was second generation Irish and traced her family ancestry to the old country on her father's and mother's side.

160

The estimated time of arrival of the baby was March 17th, an easy date to remember. The pains were not so severe, but Jonna phoned the doctor anyway about what to do next. He suggested that she get herself to the Bronxville hospital, check in, and await his arrival. She was put in a semi-private room with another young woman also awaiting the birth of her baby. Although Jonna was many hours away from birthing, she was sedated and didn't remember anything after that. True to their claim, she didn't experience any birth pains and knew nothing. Actually, she woke up the next day, March 18th and was told she had a baby boy. He was brought in the room to meet his Mama for the first time. She gingerly unwrapped the receiving blanket he was tightly wrapped in, and saw her newborn; this was the first time Jonna had ever held a baby. When the nurse came in the room to check, she chastised Jonna and told not to unwrap the baby again! He was brought back soon and was put on her breast to start the flow of milk which "came in" a couple of days later.

Although the actual birth was painless, Jonna was experiencing an uncomfortable sensation and pain in the birthing area. She was sore and did her share of complaining. The nurse instructed her about washing the area, which would increase healing. Her breasts hurt too. Sheesh, she began to feel like a cry baby. Her roommate Linda Kramer also had a baby boy on the same day, a few hours earlier. He was named Russell. She seemed much more confident and able to handle the whole birth thing. Jonna and Linda exchanged contact information and promised to keep in touch and get together after the babies could be taken outdoors.

They became good friends and shared many good times during their get-togethers over the following years. Linda was the first friend Jonna had and she cherished the friendship that lasted many years until the present day.

The Apartment

Jonna stayed in the hospital for four days. On the fourth day and just before her departure, the baby was circumcised at the hospital by her pediatrician, not for religious reasons, but for sanitary reasons. She didn't have strong feelings one way or the other, so she just went along with what the doctors recommended at that time.

According to tradition of Ashkenazic Jews (Jews of central and Eastern European origin), a new baby in the family should be given the name of a deceased beloved relative. Paul's father had passed several years before; his name was Abraham. Rachel, Paul's mother, indicated that the baby's name should start with an "A" in honor of his grandfather.

However, in the Sephardic tradition (Jews of Iberian or Middle Eastern origin) it is common for families to name their children after a living relative. This is because when it comes to the naming of a child within the Sephardim, the emphasis is typically on honoring a grandparent. Many grandparents are living to witness the birth of a grandchild. It is a significant point of pride within the Sephardic tradition for a grandparent to not only witness his or her grandchild's birth, but also to honor the tribute paid by the naming ritual.

Jonna was torn between making Rae happy and making her mother happy. Marie told her to name the baby boy Daniel. As strange as it may seem, this name was to be after the character in the movie "Ocean's Eleven:" Danny Ocean, was played by Frank Sinatra of course! Although that may not seem like a natural segue for naming Jonna's firstborn, it made perfect sense to Marie.

Trying to accommodate Marie and possibly her last wishes, Jonna named the new baby Daniel Allen Spector; the Allen was a consolation name for Rae. Maybe Jonna felt a little defiant and not ready to have her life dictated by unfamiliar customs and traditions.

The apartment had been arranged to accommodate the new baby; the "L" part of the studio had a porta crib, a changing table, a small dresser, a bassinette and a space for the carriage. The top-of-the-line carriage, called a pram, was mostly used by city dwellers to walk their babies on sidewalks in all sorts of weather.

When Danny was about a week old, Jonna walked to Montefiore Hospital and met Marie outside the front entrance; she had been hospitalized for a few days getting treatment. She wasn't necessarily thrilled about meeting her grandson, although Marie wasn't necessarily thrilled about much in those days; she was pretty worn down and rarely smiled or showed enthusiasm for anything.

One morning, a couple of months later, Cousin Bea called and suggested that she and Jonna take a ride out to the newly opened World's Fair exposition at Flushing Meadows-Corona Park in Queens, NYC.

The 1964-65 world's fair held over 140 pavilions, 110 restaurants, for 80 nations, 24 US states, and over 45 corporations to build exhibits and attractions. The immense fair covered 646 acres on half the park, with numerous pools or fountains, and an amusement park with rides near the lake. The fair's theme was "Peace Through Understanding" dedicated to "Man's Achievement on a Shrinking Globe in an Expanding Universe." American companies dominated the exposition as exhibitors. The theme was symbolized by a 12-story high, stainless steel model of the earth called the Unisphere, built on the foundation of the Perisphere at the 1939 World's Fair. The fair ran for 2 six-month seasons, April-October 1964 and April-October 1965. The admission price for adults in 1964 was $2.00 that would be equivalent to $16.69 in 2020 and $2.50 in 1965 and equivalent to $20.53 in 2020.

The fair was noted as a showcase of mid-20th century American culture and technology. The nascent Space Age, with its vista of promise, was well represented. More than 51 million attended, somewhat short of the hoped-for 70 million. It remains a touchstone for many American Baby Boomers who visited the optimistic exposition as children, before the turbulent years of the Vietnam War and many cultural changes.

It seemed ironic to Jonna that 25 years earlier, in 1939, Grandpa Al, Grandma Carmela and her mother Marie may have walked in her same footsteps at the fair!

It was an amazing expo, something like going to Disney Land or Epcot for the first time. So much to see and digest and so little time in just a day.

Little Danny was getting hungry and Jonna's breasts told her it was time for a feeding. In those years, it was uncommon to see a mother nursing an infant in public, especially in the States. A baby blanket slung over her shoulder and lightly covering the baby, provided enough privacy and was socially acceptable. So, the little fellow got his lunch in the shadow of the huge Unisphere after Jonna had a couple of small cups of the warm Sake. When she first saw the sign advertising that Sake was sold here… she said to Bea "what is SAKE?" pronounced with the hard "E" like it is spelled. Bea knew about the Japanese rice wine and corrected her with the proper pronunciation. Jonna felt a bit foolish; she had so much to learn about everything.

Endings and Beginnings

It's the way of the world and existence as far as we know. We are gifted with life, spend years as a child absorbing everything around us like sponges, then become teenagers when hormones are active and we think we know everything, moving into and through our twenties still optimistic and hopeful, then an adult in our thirties, still testing the waters of life and exploring possibilities. For the next thirty years or so we develop careers, have a family, build a business or a good job, engage in developing relationships. If our health holds out, the aforementioned scenario is as good as it gets for most people.

Others may not have such a smooth ride; they may endure major interruptions or set-backs or personal tragedies. Others coast along, with minimal expectations, and manage to get through living an existence of quiet desperation. Most are swept up in the mundane drudgery of day-to-day life and have very little to be joyous about.

Although Jonna did not have a formal education, she was gifted with logical thinking. Her training and natural inclination was to put others before herself, their needs, desires, likes and dislikes. She was there to fill in their gaps. As a small example, a jar of peanuts contains some broken and some full pieces. Jonna would eat the broken half peanuts saving the unbroken ones for others. Maybe not the best example, but you the reader, might get the picture.

Jonna did not need much in a material way, but sought to nurture her soul. She was curious, adventurous, interested and eager to explore and learn. Being married was stifling, being a caregiver was stifling, being a parent was stifling and on and on. At the time, she didn't recognize any of this and muddled through, trying to keep her boat on an even keel. That being said, she rarely looked back and went up to the plate hoping for a base hit, if not a home run.

One day in mid-June of 1964 she heard a knock on the door. To her surprise, Marie was standing in the hallway and had come for a visit. She had called a cab and was driven the several blocks from her apartment to see Jonna and her grandson. She looked awful and Jonna couldn't figure out how she had the strength and energy to make even the short trip. Jonna took a picture of Marie sitting in the loveseat, holding baby Danny.

After visiting for a while, Marie started to shake violently. Jonna took her temperature which registered 105 degrees, dangerously high. She immediately bundled up Danny, and took Marie straight to the hospital. Afterward Jonna dropped the baby off at Aunt Marge's house to babysit while Jonna returned to the hospital to see how things were going. Marie had been put in room and drugged up to the max, the pain was that intense. Jonna tried to communicate, but Marie had only final words to say, "I wish it was just an hour before I die." Jonna figured that it meant that she would only suffer for one more hour. In her mind Jonna said good-bye, and left the hospital. She picked up Danny and went to Grandma's house to attend to things there.

A couple of hours later, the phone rang with the news. Marie had died and arrangements had to be made for her remains. Grandma cried; this was the second daughter she lost to disease. Jonna was relieved that suffering ended for Marie and the rest of the family. There were no previous plans made and Jonna had to make arrangements for the Oberg-Bedell Funeral Home to pick Marie up and transport her to Staten Island for the service; there was a place for Marie to be buried in the Ocean View Cemetery, also on Staten Island.

Grandma requested an open coffin so she could see Marie for the last time. The mortician did a very good job in restoring Marie's face to resemble her in healthier days. Jonna couldn't handle a 3-day wake at the funeral home and requested a next day burial. Family and friends were notified and arranged to attend for just that one day. Even Dominic visited, showing his respect and grieving the loss. There was little time to mourn. Although Jonna felt relief in some ways, she was also saddened to think that she would not have her mother to share moments in the rest of her life. A brother from the local congregation of Jehovah's Witnesses in Staten Island gave a brief eulogy highlighting God's promise of a resurrection to life here on earth when the heavenly Kingdom would direct its attention to the earth and eventually restore it to a paradise.

Marie was laid to rest, as they say, in a burial plot that had been purchased by Grandpa Al years ago. Mourners offered their condolences and gradually the grounds were almost deserted, save for Jonna.

Jonna went through the motions by rote, in a state of semi-numbness. Her memory has surely faded to gray. There was no time to digest the situation, she had to push on, make decisions, and attend to the remaining matters at hand. Namely, Grandma still needed her.

Let's Summarize

Beatlemania hit the US in a huge way in 1963 and by 1964, after their appearance on the Ed Sullivan Show, they became the first group to have the top 5 recordings to hit the air waves at the same time. Their popularity grew exponentially and they were performing concerts all over the world. In Jonna's world, they were belting out their hit recordings: Can't Buy Me Love, Twist and Shout, She Loves You, I want to Hold Your Hand and Please Please Me on her small kitchen radio. The Beatles recordings dominated the airways for quite a while, while the teenage fans yelled and screamed during their live performances. It was the start of a revolution, not only in music, but in dress and attitude change that swept the world, especially with the beginning of the war in Viet Nam when all bets were off and controversy escalated with protestors and dissidents showing anti-war slogans and sentiments.

Danny's room (alcove) and crib were right next to the kitchen and the poor little fellow was subject to the constant strains of the recording hits of the day; believe it or not, he actually slept through the noise! I suppose the melodies of Brahms or the other classics would have been more soothing, but Jonna didn't think about that at the time. She was bopping along to the Elton John's recording of "Crocodile Rock" and all the other hits of the 60's.

The "make love not war" generation was blooming and the drug culture was in full swing. It was a time when young and old alike were questioning the status quo in government, religion and the "establishment" in general. Jonna was not among those protestors, she was born just before the baby boomers came of age and wasn't about to join the fray of the discontent. Besides, she was quite busy with the responsibilities of marriage, motherhood, caregiver and other pressing issues of day-to-day life, although she recognized that the traditional mores of a bygone era were quickly slipping away. However, she took refuge in her belief system that acknowledged God, in His due time, would reconcile and bring a reckoning to the evil and destructive forces here on earth, ultimately establishing a righteous Kingdom where justice would prevail, and fear, suffering and death would be a thing of the past, "the former things having passed away."

In the meantime, on her own home front after Marie passed, Grandma Carmela was still in need of almost daily assistance. The arrangement of taking care of two households began to look dismal and unsustainable. When Danny was 7 ½ months old, Jonna became pregnant again and that's when she started to entertain the idea of getting a larger apartment that would accommodate both Grandma and her growing family. Plans were in the making and Paul agreed that it would be a good decision. Grandma contributed her social security benefit to the household budget in exchange for living space and care. It seemed like a win-win situation all around.

After reluctantly letting go of the apartment on Rochambeau Avenue, they rented a two-bedroom garden apartment in Hartsdale, just off Central Avenue. The apartment complex was very convenient to shopping and all other services in addition to which it was just a few miles away from White Plains. Jonna doesn't remember the details of the move since

Paul took care of relinquishing the two apartments and reorganizing the furnishings that were kept. Most of Grandma's old classic furniture didn't really fit in with the new surroundings. Some pieces were given away and a few made the cut. Paul insisted that Grandma's hygiene issues be addressed immediately and that's when Jonna began giving her Gram weekly showers and grooming.

Cousin Bea was a godsend for Jonna. She visited regularly, baby sat for Danny on many occasions and generally was happy to help out where she could. They grew pretty close during those years and Bea was the closest thing to an older sister that Jonna could imagine.

It came time for Jonna to deliver her new baby. She was retaining a lot of fluid in her ankles, something that never happened before. The doctor strongly suggested she go on a quick diet and shed the extra water weight. She did so by eliminating carbohydrates and minimizing food intake altogether. Her next appointment with the doctor showed that she had lost 10 lbs in 3 ½ weeks. However, the new baby was slow to enter the world; as it turned out, he arrived 2 weeks past her due date!

Again, Jonna was at odds with naming the new boy. She just couldn't pick out a name beginning with the letter A that she liked except for Andrew and so it was. Andrew Christopher joined Jonna's world. His older brother Danny was just about 16 months old and had his own interpretation of Andrew's name. He couldn't say Andrew... so Jonna decided to call him Andy which would have been easier to pronounce. That didn't work well either and Danny kept saying Anie. The name caught on and from then the family called him Anie too. Paul was one to give nicknames to everyone; and so Andrew became Anie Anie and Ossie Goopie. As of this writing, in 2021, everyone in the family still calls him by the nickname, Anie.

When Andrew was about 3 or 4 months old, Jonna came down with strep throat. Cousin Bea was also having the same recurring problem. The antibiotics were not working well and after several tries the doctors recommended that she have a tonsillectomy. The following month, Bea and Jonna made arrangements to have their tonsils removed on the same day and at the same hospital, Fordham Hospital in the Bronx.

Unlike other surgeries where one lays down for the procedure and is medicated so that there is no pain, this surgery was performed on awake patients sitting in a chair in an upright position; it looked somewhat like what you might think of as an electric chair. Jonna was the first to be called in for the operation. A local anesthetic was administered by long needles directly into the infected area, barbaric if nothing else. Jonna felt tugging and pulling in the area, but no specific pain. Afterward she was wheeled back down to the room where the next victim awaited the procedure. That next victim was Bea who looked at Jonna with anticipation.... Like how did it go? Not wanting to create fear, Jonna gave her the "thumbs up" indicating that it was a breeze! Ha, ha, ha, the whole experience was not a breeze, especially as the anesthetic started to wear off. It hurt a lot!

When Bea was wheeled back to the room, she gave Jonna "dagger eyes." Forget about ice cream therapy, they couldn't get anything passed their throats, not even ice water! They spent an uncomfortable night in the hospital and the next couple of days proved to be equally uncomfortable and really painful. The worst part for Bea was that she couldn't smoke!

Back home, Paul had hired an Israeli nurse to attend to the care of the family during those days of healing. It seems as though adults have a much more difficult time recovering than do children. Since those days, about 55 years ago, tonsillectomies and appendectomies, immunizations, and commonly used antibiotics are not being pushed as they were then. The medical field has morphed once again and so-called helpful operations and practices have been dropped or drastically modified; it has come a long way from the days of blood-letting as a treatment to cure illnesses. "Caveat emptor," let the buyer beware!!!

The House on Chaucer Street

They had no sooner settled in to the apartment, when Paul announced that they were buying a house. He thought that paying rent was a waste of money. He found a delightful little house in the neighborhood called Poet's Corner in Hartsdale. Jonna was not privy to the actual transaction of buying the house; Paul was of the mindset that he would take care of all of that; he was the wheeler dealer after all. Grandma Rae must have helped with the down payment. Jonna's area of expertise was caregiver and manager of household duties at that time. There was no consulting about the decision to buy, but he did give her a chance to see the house before the actual purchase and closing.

The 26 streets in Poet's Corner are all named for famous poets like Longfellow, Keats and Chaucer. The neighborhood homes are a mix of styles with everything from Cape Cods to ranches, Tudors and colonials. It also encompasses 2 working farms on Secor Road that sell local produce, flowers, baked goods, honey, etc. At that time, Jonna knew the family that owned one of the farms, the Polidoros, who attended the local Kingdom Hall of JW's. Dave Polidoro was one of the Elders who served at the Hall.

Jonna immediately fell in love with the charming house situated on 1/3 acre of property abutting state land along the newly completed Sprain

Brook Parkway. There were miles of trails for playing and biking and hiking. If she remembers correctly, the cost of the house was about $24,000. Off the small entryway lay the kitchen to the right with a breakfast nook, a living room to the left and a set of stairs up to the two bedrooms and full bath. Off the kitchen, a door opened up to a stairway leading to the basement that had a finished playroom and laundry room to the left. The previous owners housed a pony in an attached, dirt-floored long stall area off the rear patio. Neighborhood ordinances didn't allow farm animals to occupy any part of the property, so when complaints came to the attention of the local constabulary, the owners decided to sell the house and move to a more rural area upstate. Grandma occupied the small bedroom upstairs, Jonna and Paul had the other larger bedroom. The house was small, but sufficient enough for the family of 5. The boys had the playroom for a bedroom that opened up to the backyard, furnished with bunkbeds and a bunch of toys and furniture for young kids. Danny was almost 2 1/2 years old and Anie Anie was a little over 1 . Thinking back about those years Jonna recalls how easy it was to raise those boys. Their personalities, although different from one another, were easily directed. They were 15 months apart, almost like Irish twins!

Grandma Carmela was having difficulty navigating the stairs to the upstairs bedroom; she took them real slow. Her chronic heart condition was becoming noticeably more debilitating during the next several months, but she managed to hang on for a while longer.

After only a few months in the house, Jonna got word that uncle Jerry died from a heart attack. He had suffered through a previous attack, but this new one took him down. The year was 1966; he was in his mid to late fifties. Grandma must have been heartbroken at this news, although it was hard to tell. Maybe she was just numb with grief with the realization that she outlived 3 of her 4 children. The funeral and final resting place was in Staten Island, the Lancona family's original home ground.

One afternoon, Jonna was sitting out front of the house and noticed a marching army of what looked like ants, headed for a crack in the cement, some of them had wings. Guess it was time to call an exterminator when they learned that in fact, they were not ants but termites! The exterminator pointed out the very noticeable mud tunnels along the wooden beams that rested on the soil inside the house. Treatment was forthcoming; the process included drilling holes all around the perimeter of the house both on the inside and outside and injecting the pesticide deep into the earth. Jonna got a lesson on termite behavior; she was told that the termites needed to return to the moisture of the earth to survive, breed and digest the cellulose in the wood. Welcome to the new house!

And the hits just kept on coming. Grandma's labored breathing became of concern and Jonna called an ambulance and had her brought to the hospital in White Plains. The doctors reported that she was suffering from congestive heart failure with water on the lungs. Some measures were taken to relieve the water accumulation, but it became clear in a day or so that her heart was giving out and she was not going to recover. She passed on November 1, 1967 at 82 years old; her funeral and burial were on Staten Island next to her husband Grandpa Al.

Jonna's family had dwindled down and only Aunt Marge, Cousins Bea, Gerald and Dennis remained nearby. Uncle Sam (Salvatore) had escaped the confines of New York several years before to seek his fortune in the warmth and sunshine of California. Jonna made efforts to keep in touch through writing letters and sending small gifts to her cousins. It wasn't that many years later that Uncle Sam also died of heart issues, the details of which Jonna doesn't remember since they had been estranged and noncommunicative for a long time and information from that quarter was not forthcoming.

Life in the house on Chaucer was busy enough through the next several years. Paul decided to put in an above-the-ground swimming pool. It had a cedar-stained deck all around, a fence, and a gate that swung up for safety. Jonna gave the boys some rudimentary swimming instruction and it was amazing how they took to the water like fish, like they were born to swim. They did flips, twists and various dives including cannon balls off the diving board. We are talking little kids here!

Cousin Bea often came over after work and she and Jonna spent time in the late evening sitting poolside, drinking wine, listening to Karen Carpenter sing… "Why do birds suddenly appear, every time you are near, just like me they long to be close to you…." Jonna tried to teach Bea to swim in the shallow end, but she just didn't get the hang of it. She would be a non-swimmer for the rest of her life. Paul and Jonna arranged a few pool parties and bar-b-que gatherings over the next few years. These were still the fairly good times.

Jonna wanted to have a family pet, so the kids would be used to animals and have no fear of them. She bought a miniature, pure-bred black poodle that fit the bill. They named her Gigi. Gigi was a little bit over a year old and in her second heat. A friend they knew had a male, full-bred black mini poodle too and arrangements were made for the two willing pups to mate. They were allocated to the "honeymoon suite" in the playroom and hopefully would do their thing. Which they did! A few months later, Jonna, acting as mid-wife, helped Gigi deliver 5 tiny babies in the upstairs bedroom. They looked like blind mice. One was not breathing… Jonna towel dried the pup and gently rubbed the skin, palpated the heart area, and miracle of miracles the baby began breathing. The pups found a teat and began nursing in short order. The stud owner got the pick of the litter, Paul's sister Dorothy took one of the pups and Jonna sold the remaining three.

The plot of Jonna's story-line was taking turns that she was ill equipped to deal with or understand. She became pregnant two more times that ended in miscarriage. The first one was extracted by a D&C procedure after 3 ½ months with no heartbeat. The second also had no heartbeat at 3 1/2 months but she would carry the dead fetus for almost the term of a normal pregnancy. Around the 8th month, Jonna went into labor and passed the mass with little effort or discomfort. However, she was worn out and anemic from the two back-to-back pregnancies. Too much, too soon.

Paul's business activities seemed to take most of his time and he was often unavailable. One day he told Jonna he was going out of town for a week to take care of some of this business. She asked about it but was told that she didn't need to know. She was really uncomfortable with this circumstance and Jonna began to question Paul's extracurricular activities and so-called businesses. He said Italian women are good with staying home, taking care of children and domestic duties while the husbands were free to explore their life as they saw fit. Something was fishy, but Paul assured her that as long as he was able to give her money for household expenses, nice vacations and getaways she should be content and give him unquestioned leeway. His take on their situation was that if he provided her with a car and enough money to maneuver, she didn't really need him for more; that assessment was probably quite true.

Her saving grace was that she was involved with the Witnesses during this time and had a good friend to hang-out with. Debbie F. and her Mom Alba R. became her go to family. They offered some stability, and Jonna was happy to be around them. Meeting attendance, daily text readings and preparation for service helped ease the pain of her distress. But her unease grew as Paul was missing from the scene often and not very much interested in her portion of life. At least she was financially provided for and not physically abused. Although emotional abuse was just as devastating as she would later come to understand. She took good care of the house, the children, shopping, cleaning, cooking and the rest; what was there to complain about. As time passed Jonna began to realize that Paul let her make family matter decisions and other routine decisions without question as it gave him the freedom to do his own thing and not be accountable to her. She suspected there were other women in his life on a regular basis, which turned out to be quite true.

Jonna was angry, and began to harbor vengeful thoughts to "get back" at Paul. This proved to be even more stressful, since that kind of behavior was contrary to her nature. She felt desperate and began to make desperate choices and foolish behavior.

There are too many incidents to relate in a cohesive fashion. Needless to say, Jonna reacted poorly and her distrust and suspicion began to eat away at her composure. She was terribly unhappy and tried to think of ways to mitigate the stressful situation. Perhaps a move to another area would be a solution; a new environment without the current influences in his life might make a difference. Maybe if he got away from his involvement with the mob and the other women there would be changes and they could lead a more normal life. She forgot the old adage, "wherever you go, there YOU are." But at least it could be a new start, with new experiences and living conditions, maybe things would be better.

The story goes deep and wide from this point forward for Jonna and her children and thank goodness for the children. Jonna was hardly more than a kid herself and loved growing up with her sons. She took them to carnivals, beaches, museums, visits to the Statue of Liberty and innumerable other excursions, trips and events. The kids had lots of freedom to explore the safe neighborhood. Unexpected twists and turns marked the future, almost as if they were predestined or maybe beyond her control. Some things just weren't meant to be she found out as the future years developed and unfolded. Her youth, indefatigable optimism and enthusiasm for life kept her going through what one might call even rougher times ahead. Jonna didn't know enough to step back and let the marriage play out. Instead, she was trying to fix the situation.

Grandma Carmela and Jonna, 1958.

Jonna, 19 years old.

Last picture of Marie holding Danny, June 1964.

Jonna. Chaucer St house 1966.

Jonna, 1958, up at the park.

Paul, Danny and Anie. Chaucer St house.

Paul and Jonna, Danny and Anie Ft Lauderdale, Florida, circa 1969.

Anie and Danny at play park, 1969.

Afterward

More than a half century has passed since the marriage years and Jonna can reflect more objectively. Her reflections on her early history hopefully benefits and entertains readers, especially Jonna's family and friends. Insight does not give meaning to life, but does provide perspective. If anything, she has learned to be gentler and kinder to herself. She no longer feels desperate and does not act out of desperation, but coasts along, living in the moment, enjoying the process.

Jonna has never been competitive in nature. She doesn't pit herself against the accomplishments of others; rather, she sets personal goals and you might say lives in her own world.

Other than the diminished health that accompanies 78 years on earth, Jonna is content with small accomplishments. Writing this memoire has been a few years in the making, with many starts and stops along the way, as they say "a labor of love." She recognizes that she may never be great at any one thing, but that's ok. Being pretty good at most things will have to suffice.

About The Author

Life has been good to Jeanne-Marie in many ways. She enjoyed many learning opportunities and endeavors. Early on she helped start a family painting and decorating business with her two sons and another partner. She started another business selling and installing roofing and siding throughout Rockland County. In New York, she obtained a real estate license. In Florida, she obtained a Series 7 license to sell stocks and bonds. She edited the monthly newsletter of the Adirondack Hiking Club; the hiking trip to Ireland was fantastic. The many courses in art, interior design and architectural studies, through Marymount College in Tarrytown, NY, Parsons School of Design and NYU sharpened her skills. Painting workshops in the US and Europe enhanced her focus. Over the years, she traveled throughout the US, Italy and France broadening her perspective about life and art. Creativity and art have sustained her, writing her latest challenge. Jeanne-Marie remains inquisitive and open to life, even in her older years.

She lives in Silver City, New Mexico, with her husband Don.

Made in United States
North Haven, CT
07 February 2023

32190764R00124